Same Skirt Different Day

A Camino Chronicle

BY THE SAME AUTHOR

Patrick and the Cat Who Saw Beyond Time
Memoir: Book One — The Tiger and the Taxi Driver
Memoir: Book Two — The Tiger and the Taxi Driver
The Road to Delphi — A Gentle Mystery

Same Skirt Different Day

A Camino Chronicle

Nigelle de Visme

DEDICATION

First to my Pilgrim Feet, thank you for carrying me.

In equal measure, heartfelt thanks to Caroline, Jeff, Joe, Johanna, Thérèse and Tina for your very blessed gifts.

And to Macabi, Merrell and Michelin 160, that most slender and fulsome of Camino Guides, NOK and 1000mile Socks, thanks beyond thanks for each of your perfections.

CONTENTS

PROLOGUE

April 5th 2014 – Countdown 5 weeks

I'm on the first step to the longest walk of my life, me, who was told I would never walk again. The wheelchair belongs to a different world now and if I reach the end of this walk I suspect my feet will be stronger than anyone believed possible. Homer emailed to say he knew I could do it; he should know, he's the Chinese wonder-worker who worked on my feet independently of the dire predictions of the Australian medical fraternity. He knew I would walk again when I and all the doctors seeing me at the Ipswich General shook their heads over the Xrays of my feet and pronounced me wheelchair bound forever. That was not so far back in Dreamtime. It took four years for me to walk without thinking about how to walk, and after living almost forty years in Australia I came home to England, to a small town in Somerset, a town with a great history of myth and legend and tragedy – Glastonbury. The Camino idea came left of field.

To begin with I rescue a pair of grand walking boots from the boot of my car. I had bought them in fit of fitness five years back just in case I was tempted to walk in Powys, the Pennines or do a couple of miles of the South Coast Walk. I've never been tempted, but the boots, Ecco, feel fine and off I walk.

I start by daily puffing and wheezing my way up Glastonbury Tor. And then up and down, up and down, back to back, twice daily. It doesn't come easily to me this kind of physical effort. What I really need are long flat distances. I discover the magic on my doorstep. The RSPB has a bird reserve at Ham Wall and English Nature has Shapwick Heath – a continuing walk of many miles linked across a small B road, a walk accessible starting from my front door.

It is now March 2014. Slowly I build up to three hours walking a day, thrilling to the boom of the bitterns in the reeds, the dawn mists over the mere, where Arthur heard the dying of the day as the Ladies of the lake bore him through the mists to Avalon, and the silence. From my front door the return distance is around 8 miles, about 13 kilometres. One day I attempt four hours – and hit a problem. My feet have swollen, the middle toes jam against their respective boot and I can barely hobble home. I phone Caroline on Gozo whose Camino five years ago, at the same age I am now, was a pilgrimage of pain: blisters, two new knees, new hip. *Buy the next size boot,* she advises, *part of my problem,* she says*, was not being told to do just that.*

I buy a pair of high ankled walking boots, soft, wide and very supportive, with only a little bit of leather, no need to 'break them in' for a year or two. They are walk out of the shop comfortable. The shop itself is a wonder; it opened in Street two months past and is the only Merrell's Outlet in the whole of England, Wales and Scotland. Imagine that for a stroke of good fortune, right on my doorstep. I am researching everything now: socks and wool, silk liners or not, blisters, compeed, Vibram soles (my boots have them), Gore-Tex for waterproofing (my boots have that too, blisters are caused, my research tells me, by wet socks as well as friction), gaiters, NOK (a French miracle; urban legend holds that the French don't get blisters because they use this specially developed lubricant); then the dilemma – to lubricate or not to lubricate. It's a controversial topic which runs across whole websites. When in doubt, it seems at this point in my preparations, I can always turn to the local *ungüento peregrinos*. The Spanish have had centuries of dealing with pilgrim feet problems, I can rely on that. I spend hours walking and hours researching. Blisters are my Fear. I will walk short distances, my Camino will be a prayer not a performance, but *blisters* – oh dear.

I tie red and white polka dot ribbon to everything, wide ribbon on the rucksack, and narrow ribbon on camera, camera case, wash bag, both skirts, both boots, torch, walking stick, fleece zip, waterproof jacket zip, sleeping bag zip, whatever I can tie a ribbon to. I glue a strip of ribbon to the camera charger, another strip to the cover of my Michelin Guide. If I forget something then the cheery white polka dots on scarlet ribbon will act as a mnemonic. *Ah*, someone will say, *I know who's left this behind.* I shall be such a slow walker they'll catch up with me. My gay and brave polka dots will define Everything with a sense of These Belong To Me, Thank You Sooooooo Much For Returning Them.

The only way to Spain without flying from the other side of England is Bristol to Paris, Paris to Bilbao and by bus from Bilbao the following day to Pamplona, then the evening bus to Roncesvalles. EasyJet determines the flight by cost and I take a quiet pleasure in seeing the significance of the date – May 13th. Father Bede will surely shower his blessings as I step out; it was the day he left planet earth for his ultimate Journey.

CONTEMPLATIONS

Pilgrim Feet are Precious – Signs and Wonders

The Camino. I've known of it forever and over the years met a number of women and men who have walked it. The Camino refers to the ancient pilgrimage route that begins at the Spanish border of Roncesvalles and threads its way through the Cathedral cities of Pamplona, Logroño, Burgos, León and Astorga to the great Cathedral of Santiago de Compostela, a distance of nearly five hundred miles to traverse. Like all the other routes it has its own name or two, the Camino de Santiago, the Camino Francés, but so famous is it that just calling it The Camino is enough. The four main routes from France that converge more or less at St Jean Pied de Port have their own names; each of the four major Portugese routes has its own name. The Spanish routes are multiple, each having its own name too: Camí de San Jaume from Montserrat near Barcelona, the Ruta de Tunel from Irun, the Camino Primitivo from Bilbao and Oviedo, the Camino de Levante from Valencia and Toledo. There is the old English route from Ferrol, the Camino Inglés; the Via de la Plata from Seville and Salamanca; Camino Aragonés; Camino del Norté and so on. But I'm going to walk The Camino, the one that everyone knows. And the secret truth is – I don't know why. To give my feet a fighting chance I won't begin in France. I doubt the Spanish hop over the border to start their Camino in St Jean Pied de Port anyway.

In more sombre moments I wake, usually at four o'clock in the morning, and quake with fear at the enormity of what I am proposing my dear little broken feet will have to do. It may be my last walk ever. If I disappear along the way, and people often do, there are little shrines to them, then it will be a most fitting departure - my whole life has been a pilgrimage; the alone to the Alone sums it up nicely. I have always been a pilgrimette.

I pack and repack before leaving, hone my needs to minimal, one skirt to walk in and one skirt to rest in, one pair of boots to walk in and one pair of sandals to rest in. Two tops, a hat and a cap, a good poncho, a down sleeping bag, sundries and toiletries. A friend offers me a very old Nikon coolpix which he repaired, I buy a battery charger, a spare battery, pack it safely. Should I take poles? Or no poles? My lack of coordination since the wheelchair is laughable – I will compromise, take a single walking stick to balance me on slippery slopes. I spend weeks researching why, according to urban legend, the French don't get blisters and I finally discover, by reading an interview in that marvellous online Women-on-the-Road e-letter, the French Miracle – NOK. In the process of that essential research I discover the guarantee-no-blisters 1000mile socks too, made in England. My feet will be anointed and swaddled all the Way.

1000mile socks are the English secret; a phone conversation with Karen of 1000mile socks convinces me. I order a pair and as soon as they arrive go off for a long walk. To my horror my chubby little legs balloon. The cuffs on my wonder socks are too tight. I call Karen with my tale of woe and she suggests a different style with a softer, longer cuff which she will send for me to trial. They are marvellous; fit my chubby legs in comfort. During our third conversation Karen congratulates me on my challenge and asks if I would write a blog for them.

What a thought. I feel passionately about limitations and going beyond them, about challenges, about saying yes to life with all its joys and sorrows, about women in particular, about not saying no to a small or large dream because of poverty, a constant bedfellow that bedevils me. There is (almost) always a way. Sometimes the thought of the Camino paralyses me but I use all the motivational strategies I've learned through my life to get through the *acedia* that I know catches everyone off guard from time to time. *Solvitur ambulando* – it is solved by walking. I will walk the Camino to walk through the sorrows of my life, to leave a smile in my wake. I say Yes to Karen. *A little background*, she asks, and I reduce a not quite ordinary life of an ordinary middle-aged woman with her mannerisms to a few pages.

My skirt is a stroke of genius. As a woman of a certain age, almost septuagenarian, loo stops are an imperative part of route planning. I doubt I'll find many conveniences along the Meseta. I've never cross-dressed – jeans included – but finding a skirt to walk in for nearly 500 miles is a challenge. Available online are slim fitting things, so-called safari wear, short, tight and only suitable for a skeleton on a cat-walk. My travel angel leads me across the Pond to the marvel of Macabi. An American secret. This garment will never grace a catwalk, but for a walk along El Camino it must be the most marvellous invention ever designed by a woman, for women. Loose, semi-elastic waisted with a drawstring too, virtually instant drying, sturdy, deep pocketed with a secret zippered pocket inside one of its deeper pockets in which goes passport, pilgrim passport, cash. Inside the other deepest of pockets is a tiny hidden pocket exactly the size of a credit or debit card. In the pockets proper go camera, Michelin Guide, notebook, pencil, water bottle sometimes, food sometimes; the perfect Franciscan Pockets. The skirt loops up, dresses down, dresses up. A skirt of many talents; the perfect garment for discretion.

I practise a few walks. I can bounce along the road from Glastonbury to Street and back happily, a total of five miles, and do it a few times a week. I can manage the eight miles to

Wells along the droves too, yet I find to my dismay that when I attempt real walks I flounder badly. I don't know why. I am not in pain, my feet are fine, my Merrell boots a joy to walk in. My body doesn't want to obey my mind – or is it the other way round?

One day I make myself walk the RSPB path along Ham Wall Reserve and continue on through Shapwick Heath. At the end I sit and eat a banana and wonder how on earth I will retrace my steps home. I have to, of course, but as I finally leave the Reserve my left hip baulks like a donkey at a ditch. The thigh muscle collapses; I can't walk home. I have done eight miles before I reach the drove where a van is parked. I crawl up to the man in a van, tap on his window and whimper: *I can't walk home! You wouldn't happen to be going to Glastonbury would you ...?* He is.

My GP says it is a muscular thing normally associated with people who sit down a lot. Could he be speaking of writers and artists and thinkers? I smile. He's walked the Appalachian Trail. There are a couple of decades between us, but he gives me confidence. My Chinese acupuncturist spends an hour and a half applying acupressure, acupuncture, herbal oils, massage and a sort of rolfing technique and says firmly: *No Walking, you have no muscle! Must rest, let repair.*

I am not amused. No walking? Hulloooooo. He collects his eyebrows from the ceiling as I tell him 500 *miles* of walking is on the cards...

Otherwise I'm in fine fettle. My Barmah Ladies Drover hat arrives from Townsville Hatters, a gift from Thérèse. I love it. The sides are of waterproof webbing, the brim and crown of waterproofed canvas and it sports an Aboriginal scarf; a nod to my love of that land. A friend here takes a pre-pilgrimage photo; I feel a mite pretentious in such pristine headgear. A battered hat is more the order of the Way but I'm sure the

Way will oblige by and by. I paint a small cockleshell with the traditional red cross of St James and attach it to the Aborigine scarf.

Nothing looms to say No, don't go. Even my hip, which takes four weeks to return to normal, which time brings me to within ten days of my flight date, isn't quite enough to make me cancel The Plan. Too many signs and symbols appeared to convince me it is all meant to be. Now I've found NOK, 1000mile socks and Macabi I am well on my way. When I wobble other signs and wonders appear to encourage me.

My Merrell boots conjure up one of those Signs and Wonders. I notice the sole is beginning to part company with the upper and I panic that they will not last the walk. I have had them less than a fortnight. They are also the last pair in existence, old stock. I am offered another style but none fit my foot like a foot the way these do. The decision is mine and I can't make it. I take the boots home again to ponder and pray. I return the following day via the old peat beds on the Levels, a long route that requires a pee stop in a field along the way. My boots are grey with amethyst trim. As I stand up my foot moves a patch of stinging nettles and there in the middle of this field and hidden by the patch of nettles is a huge ovoid crystal, grey and amethyst. It fits in the palm of my hand, my fingers barely closing over it. How it came to be there and how my foot happened to find it and why I 'chose' *there* to pause for a pee baffles the Law of Synchronicities. I hold my happenstance find in wonder. It *is* a sign. It is fluorite and fluorite, say the shamans, is powerful healing medicine. It is associated with bones. On the wild and lonely peat bogs of the Somerset Levels is my message: Keep the boots, have them glued by the cobbler. I divert to the last real cobbler in Somerset, apprenticed by Clarks long ago and now independent. He loves my story, chuckles at the crystal, promises the boots will hold for 500 miles and more. And so they do.

Another Sign and certainly more than Wonder: when I initially contemplated the Camino I wanted a pilgrim passport from Spain or France, a dainty concertina'd *credencial*, not the clumpy booklet offered by the English CSJ. I wanted it before I left so that its first stamp would be Our Lady of Glastonbury. Glastonbury is the oldest of English pilgrimages, older even than Catholicism in England. Pilgrimages were banned after 1539 when the Taliban of their time destroyed all the beauty and grace found in the churches of Our Lady's Dowry, but with a nod to historical accuracy and a more hallowed tradition I fancy starting under the mantle of Her Grace.

I summon all the gumption Goddess has graced me with and think outside the box: I will need to find an English speaking priest in Spain and ask him to send me a Spanish *credencial*. Ha! *That is not legitimate for pilgrim passports*, comes back replies from all the monasteries I email. Pilgrims have to show up at their first departure point to be given their *credencial* duly registered with the pilgrim's passport details, signed, sealed and blessed.

No is a word that brings out the worst, or the best, in me. No? Whadya mean, No? An energy surge from Australian days. There I understood Yes, it was the word that got things done, circumvented all No's. Must be the criminal element seeping through the genes of its original settlers; not for nothing is Ned Kelly a hero Downunder. I continue my pursuit doggedly until a chink of light invites me through a different door. More research reveals an entire seminary – an *English* Seminary – in Spain. My arch enemy Henry VIII was wholly instrumental in the miracle of this story. In 1538 when all could see the writing on wall the English were invited by Philip of Spain to found a seminary in Spain and send out their young priests to study under the safe protection of Catholic Spain while Catholicism in England was being criminalised and Catholic persecution proliferated.

16

So it is to this august establishment that I direct my pilgrim plea. I select a name on its website to telephone. *An unusual request*, I am told, and not one the kindly voice said he could easily see a way to fulfilling, but, *leave it with me*, he said – and so I did.

Time passes. An email comes, asking for my passport and personal particulars. More time passes. One day I receive a slip from the Post Office asking me to take I.D. to sign for a letter. When it is passed over to me I cannot begin to anticipate what such a grand envelope, with its gold embossed monogram, holds. I am so intrigued I open it right there in front of the sorting officer. Oh my! It is a Spanish *credencial* with an accompanying letter and a map of the southern route of the Camino and other things. My feet don't remember touching pavement as I walk home and there I read the letter again. The official stamp starting my pilgrimage from the issuing monastery in Spain which my *chevalier* had approached on my behalf is Puente Duero. Puente Duero is the river St Teresa crossed to begin her Carmelite Order in Avila, a few miles from the English Seminary. St Teresa and Holy Mary initiate my Pilgrim Passport. Oh my! is all I can say again.

The podiatrist calls with a cancellation. My GP had sent a referral letter eight weeks ago for an urgent appointment. I assume a higher reality took matters in hand, or feet, to gift me this appointment five days before I leave.

The matter of my injured thigh muscle becomes clear. Not only have I a foot history of multiple fractures I have, so I discover at this late age, one leg shorter than the other which throws out my hip and back and thigh and what all. That, with a deformed walk from birth, makes walking a challenge. My feet, contrary to the common lot, supinate, my big toes have never touched earth. The good podiatrist watches my walk, measures my legs, studies my boots and gives me a wondrous pair of insoles. They aren't built up to make my legs match, but they do tilt my feet to balance my unusual walk. They feel sublimely comforting. Thank you NHS, for coming up trumps when I most need you. The head podiatrist comes in to see me: *I saw your name on the list of patients today and had to come to see how you are,* she says. I tell her I am off to walk the Camino and her eyes sparkle, she wants to see my maps and hat which are in the car. She says firmly, smiling hugely and generating shining auras of confidence around the clinic: "*you* can do this!" then: "you *can* do this, slowly, slowly!" We hug and make an approximate appointment for 3 months hence...

Last night, Maundy Thursday, I was one of the *mandatum* at the Washing of the Feet. My whole story is about feet, feet, feet. Joe sat next to me, he walked the Camino last year: *of course you'll do it,* he tells me, *just take your time. The Way will carry you.*

I fly out with bright feathers on Tuesday. The Way will carry me.

Same Skirt Different Day

1

Pamplona and the Birth of a *Peregrina*

I'm looking out of my window to the grandest view of Bilbao. Excitement finally has the edge over weeks, months actually, of apprehension, preparation and panic.

I can now begin my adventure at the beginning of my Camino with my arrival in Pamplona and my first sleep in a mixed dorm of hundreds. I decide bussing to Roncesvalles was becoming one concern too many; I didn't need it and set off to search out the first *albergue* mentioned in my Michelin Guide, *Jesus and Maria*. I'm given a ticket number, 14, and sent off to find its corresponding bunk. Leaving my rucksack there I spend the day exploring this charming town, picnicking in an attractive park, walking the ramparts and checking the cockleshells are in place enough for me to follow. But oh, the dormitory! I didn't sleep almost at all. Not even with best French beeswax earplugs could I block out the snoring and more subtle 'noise' from the energy fields around me of tired pilgrims but I was aware of my first blessing – in a dorm of over a hundred double bunks I had a lower one with no one above me.

In the shower room a Korean women is applying masks and serums, studiously staring at her face in the wall length mirror as I shower behind her. The door was unlocked so I switched off my embarrassment button and carry on regardless. I wonder if mixed showers and nude bods will be all the go from here on. Push away the thought. It is morning and barely light as I leave and retrace the little brass cockleshells embedded in the paving to follow, follow all the way to Santiago. When the town meets the country the cockleshells will become stone milestones or wooden signposts. I call them cockleshells but they are really scallop shells, the emblem of St James, Santiago.

Out of Cizur Menor a true pilgrim overtakes me. I don't yet consider myself a true pilgrim, my total walks have been an accumulation of miles to and from Wells and Glastonbury. This gentleman from Girona has a 6 foot staff, made by himself, with a cross at the top. He sports a jaunty bushy grey beard sprinkled with wildflowers from yesterday's walk, cornflowers, poppies, yellow daisies. I am charmed. He speaks, could his romantic appearance imply anything other, nine Romance languages fluently. To our mutual regret English is not one of them. Imagine an Englishman wandering the country lanes of Godalming with flowers in his beard. Yes, it *could* happen in Glastonbury but you could bet your pilgrim boots the man would also have carmine toenails and be reeling on a few unsavoury substances. This charming gentleman from Girona is the real deal. He comments on my skirt, thoroughly approves of it for a *peregrina*! I glow with the compliment and am thus promoted from pilgrimette to pilgrim, a *peregrina*.

He walks on. I am slow and I walk with measured pace toward the far mountains ahead. I walk as far as Zariquiegui, 11 kilometres. The next *albergue* is up and over Alto del Perdón 2540 feet high and down into Uterga and I know I can't do that distance, that high, on my first day. I pass vast haystacks the size of apartment blocks and learn my first lesson – never look up when climbing, it is too daunting. Instead I look down and amaze myself at seeing the sliver of white chalk path below me serpentine all the way to distant Pamplona. I have walked all that way. Actually, it was easy, tiring, but easy.

The next morning at sunrise I continue my climb. And oh! look at the colours, the beauty! It is the beginning of six weeks of dreamscape, such beauty. Puffing and panting and exhilarated I round the last upward spiralling bend to the top of Alto del Perdón to see the extraordinary metal silhouettes, larger than life-size, spanning the crest of the mountain. Most thrilling of all is the leading figure – it is a *woman*, a woman in a *skirt*! She becomes a symbol for me. I know then I will make it all the way to Santiago. The wind here is fierce, and the silhouette figures have been sculpted to show its ever presence in the flow of their garments, their hair, the tilt of the pilgrims' heads. It is a fitting place too for all the giant white windmills, but no Don Quixote to tilt at them.

I can barely leave such a scene but a further 450 miles beckons. Down a steep and rocky path I go to make the first of my many detours, five or ten miles to Eunate and the Romanesque church. I smile at my enthusiasm for adding miles to the already unimaginable distance and I keep on walking.

2

Eunate to Cirauqui

A tricky but so pretty descent from my first mountain until the flat at Uterga and on to Muruzábel. I am in good spirits, fairly bounce along, pluck honeysuckle to put in my scarf for perfume, eat a *wha whoom!* bought from Carrefore in Pamplona. I love these French crepes rolled around a filling of Nutella. I turn into the last village and ask a pretty young woman the path to Eunate. She turns at my voice, I swallow involuntarily as she touches my arm and leads me to the end of her home where another road runs left through a small green. She is blind. I thank her, lightly touching her arm too, and walk as she had directed. And walk and walk.

There is a provocative sign saying Eunate in a field ahead but no arrows. Which path shall I take? I send up a quick *Help* to Holy Mary, without much confidence I confess, there is no evidence of human habitation from where I stand. But lo and behold the sentence is barely out of my mouth when appears a tractor. I wave him to stop and shout over the engine's roar, *donde es Eunate per favor?* The driver laughs, *not another doughy pilgrim,* I can hear him thinking as he points straight ahead and then right.

A long walk, by my standards, and I am here. It is a pretty Romanesque church and the tranquillity within tangible. I sit, thankful, for some while in the presence of the Madonna in Majesty seated on the Throne of Wisdom, as all Madonnas were prior to the invention of the printing press since when we've been told what to think and how to think it. Much of what we flippantly say comes as received opinion, assumes the gravitas of the Holy Writ, *"I read it in a book, the newspaper"*, and more recently *"I saw it on TV, facebook, twitter"* and twits believe it, whatever it is.

I feel compelled to walk on to Mañeru as the famed Puente la Reina seems too big a town for my apprehension to cope with in looking for a small *albergue*. Big Mistake. I reckoned without the climb. I walk for hours alone until a woman comes towards me carrying an orchid. I ask her how far away is this elusive village of Mañeru. Well, I don't *quite* have the command of Spanish or Basque to put it so eloquently, but she understands my torture of her language and to my dismay holds up the flat of her hand to vertical and says five kilometres. Uh oh! I've already done my mountain peak and detour for the day and haven't spoken to my feet about another serious climb.

It is vertical too. I think I shall die. I have finished my water, have no fruit, my legs are wobbly. Silly me. On and on and on and up and up and up I walk to collapse at the door of an *albergue* of twelve beds in a village of fourteen houses. The owner looks at me with enormous pity, gives me two glasses of water in quick succession, but says: *completo*. I confess I burst into tears of exhaustion. She pats my hand, she'd already taken off my *mochila*, and makes a phone call. She then indicates I sit where I am and off she goes. A good ten minutes later a young man arrives and then I hear a car. This kindly woman has rustled up a temporary caretaker for her *albergue*, gone to fetch her car, picks up my *mochila* and invites me to sit in the passenger seat. She drives me miles up hill and down dale to Cirauqui, actually only another couple of kilometres and two hills, where I am welcomed by a young woman who speaks English. She smiles and says as she stamps my *credencial*: *Glastonbury? My boyfriend comes from Dorset.*

She gives me the last bunk. But my knees have died and I can't walk upstairs. Somehow, with help, I do. A young Slovenian woman watches my hobbling progress up the stairs, comes to my bunk and offers to massage my knees with a special herbal unguent from Germany. She warms her hands under running hot water before she begins. Her hands are magical and she insists I keep the cream. That cream will last me until Santiago. I will use it on my feet and knees after each day's walk. I use Lynne's gift of Thai burn-through-to-the-aching-muscle ointment on my left thigh each day too, and always the French secret, NOK, to anoint my feet each morning before swaddling them in 1000mile socks. From Cirauqui on I don't have a single twinge in either knee regardless of the mountains I will climb. There were times BC – Before Camino – when my knee would give out as I walked up Glastonbury High Street, this gift of healing is not something I gloss over.

Now I am able to walk slowly downstairs to sit on the church wall in the warmth of the setting sun. I do a double take as my charcoal skirt walks past. *Macabi!* I call, and stand up to reveal mine. Tina's pink headband hides stitches; she had fallen on that tricky but pretty descent down to Uterga; a doctor stitched her head and hand. We laugh, introduce ourselves and pose for a photograph in our charcoal skirts.

The *albergue* offers a pilgrim meal which I eat with gusto at a table with a Dutchman who has read Johanna's book – in Dutch – of her walk from Le Hague to Jerusalem. I have her gift of Our Lady of Finisterre pinned to the inside pocket of my skirt.

3

la Casa Magica and Beyond

Before I left for the Camino I read that a woman in the sacristy at Le Puy walked from there to Santiago three times; Le Puy to Santiago is 1000 miles. The third time she walked it was after a serious hip operation at the age of 74. Alexandra David-Néel, whose photo I have on my camera for a quick pick-me-up when I'm flagging, walked at least 3000 miles into and through Tibet and the Himalayas over a number of years. The French government refused to renew her passport at the age of 87, or was it 94? because by then she was a National Treasure and they didn't want her disappearing behind a snow drift somewhere beyond Zhongba. She died in 1969 aged 101, on my 13th birthday as it happened. Peace Pilgrim, between the ages of 59 to 86, clocked up 25,000 miles wearing out numberless pairs of plimsolls as she criss-crossed America. The young Slovenian angel yesterday had walked from Trinidad des Arres to Cirauqui *in one go*. *Twenty five plus miles, thirty-eight kilometres*. Exhausted, she still took time to massage my knee.

I walk as far as Villatuerta, taking the advice of the two women *hospitaleros* who were so kind yesterday and who said firmly, *do not walk more than 10 kilometres tomorrow*. Villatuerta is about ten kilometres, not a hilly walk and across the bridge I see the sign for an *albergue*. The town is so pretty, the river so clear and gurgling as it winds its way through glades, I decide to stop right here. As soon as I enter the huge door of the *albergue* and pass its unpromising exterior I am entranced. The renovation of this old warren of rooms under many layered roof heights supported by massive round beams is a visual

27

delight. Cobbled courtyard, tiled stairs, whitewashed dormitories with real beds not bunks, little individual alcoves add to its aura of charm. I choose one by a balcony with French doors, the fragrance of the jasmine *polyanthum* tumbling down the old wall outside fills the room.

La Casa Magica is ... magic. To my delight it is the one *albergue* wholeheartedly recommended to me by my Australian friend, Claire, who had set off a few weeks ahead of me. I look through the register and there is her name, with the highest recommendation written beside it. I wash my 1000mile socks and little yellow towel, its sunshine colour adds a touch of zest to the old warm walls behind the washing lines. I am introduced to a good-looking couple from Castlemaine in Victoria, Vanessa and John; they are lovely. The Canadian Lovelies Tina and Gary are also here; all manner of Lovelies are drawn to this rather special *albergue*.

The owners of la Casa Magica met while walking the Camino and came back here to create their haven for pilgrims. Dinner and breakfast, all organic, prepared and cooked lovingly, are beyond delicious. I overhear a young man at the other end of the table say as he nodded in my direction that he wished he had a video so he could show his wife he had met Judi Dench's sister. Poor JD ... it's been said before, but walking the Camino is not doing my appearance any favours now. I barely recognise my tired self.

Cherries in abundance by the river and a glamorous wedding in the old church leaves warm memories of a relaxing day and a reluctance to walk on, but I wake refreshed and ready to go. Only one other pilgrim was in my dorm, a Frenchman in the adjacent alcove. He didn't snore, and thoroughly approves of my use of NOK in the morning. He grins and brings forth a tin of l'Occitane *Roses des Quatre Reines* from his *mochila* saying also that a midday sprinkle of talcum powder on the feet is the perfect protection against blisters for longer walks. One can always rely on a Frenchman to be so specific in his preferences.

A beautiful walk over small bridges takes me through Estella, another town that appeared too large to explore for an *albergue*. I pass the thousand steps up to the church; my legs say firmly, *No!* at the thought of climbing them. I walk on two blocks, happen to glance left and to my amazement see a lift shaft ascending straight to heaven with no apparent reason for its being there at the end of an alley. An Adventure, I think, and veer off to explore it. I press the button, open the door, press another button to shoot up to the highest floor and whoosh! I am on top of the world.

Stepping out reveals a splendid panorama of the town with the mountains beyond and a long wooden walkway directing me into the back of the church. An Invitation. It just so happens Mass is on. Still wearing my *mochila* I join the queue and to my surprise the priest offering the Host says *Body of Christ* in English. I reply, as one does, and he hesitates. In a nanosecond I know why: *I am Catholic*, I smile, and he is comforted. Later he says, heavily, *There are very few Catholics in England* and I reply *I know, I'm one of the few!* I add: *and could I possibly use your loo?* He invites me into the Sacristy where I have a brainwave. *'I've not been able to access my emails,'* I say, *'and no one knows where I am, could I ask you an enormous favour? Please will you look up Our Lady of Glastonbury and send an email telling my parish that I made it to Estella?'* Many weeks later I read his email, reply and thank him.

On I walk through light forests, pausing at the Monasterio de Irache for the obligatory wine from the fountain. I top up my water bottle with it, a wise move; it gives me wings to ascend the next vertical mountain to Villamayor de Montjardin.

That vertical does it for me. I sink into a heap at the *hospitalero's* table and ask for a bed in this attractive restored

Dutch *albergue*. Well, he didn't think there were any left, but tells me to wait a moment as he disappears. Quite a while later he returns to say a young person had given up the last bed and will sleep on a mattress in the foyer. It really is a bed too, not a bunk, with gay red sheets and pillowcase. I offer my profuse thanks to all and later watch with compassion as so many other tired *peregrinos* arrive and are turned away. This is a super *albergue* with good food, lots of grace, a touch evangelical, but that is their charism.

The man across the room, from Venezuela, has walked from Roncesvalles and his knee has given out. He is in severe pain. My GP gave me an elastic knee support as mine sometimes gives out just walking up Glastonbury High Street. Instinctively I feel I won't need it along this walk, I unpack it and give it to him. His face shines with a kind of wonder and he puts it on at once. He will be able to sleep tonight, he tells me.

A ditzy Australian woman of a certain age, probably close to my own, wearing four inch high-heeled boots, shares my room. She hasn't been able to sleep because of snorers, has no earplugs. I give her a pair of mine. She thinks her rucksack weighs twenty kilograms, carries the entire range of Lancôme serums and creams, make up and perfume, but no earplugs. Time, I think, to break out my eyeliner ... but, *oh bummer!* I can't find it. The last time I used it was in Bilbao the day before I became a *peregrina* ... ah well, it'll have to go on my must buy list for Burgos.

4

Los Arcos, Torres del Rio and Fast Forward to Logroño

I ache, oh I ache. I ache in every fibre of my body, I ache from walking, I ache from carrying the world on my back (even with the absence of eyeliner) and I ache from exhaustion and sleep deprivation. If I could kill every snorer I would. Most cheerfully. There they lie, sleeping the sleep of the unjust, shaking the bunks, the floors, the very walls of the dormitories; their snoring would make piglings in a pigsty sound like Palestrina. And then they wake up – they *dare* to wake up fresh as daisies, bright eyed and bushy tailed, wondering why the rest of us lay like limp rags, scowling loudly in their direction. I'll wager all these lone men are lone because their wives are desperately trying to catch up on years and *years* of sleep deprivation. Their wives have probably *begged* them to take a Walk, a Long Walk. Yet I will soon have to confess that there are *women* snorers who are unfit for communal living too. I am about to meet three in a room for four.

Walk, eat, sleep. That's the mantra. Hot shower on arrival to ease away the worst of the aches, dress in the non-walking skirt, tomorrow's top, same petticoat, rest the feet by putting on sandals, apply the German herbal cream of different mints and rosemary; wash whatever might need washing and then go and forage for food. I begin walking at 6.00 and stop six hours later. With my wavering blood sugar ups and downs the *menu del dia* at midday suits me very well. It's always a substantial three course meal with a bottle of wine, which I swap for water, although that is also often included, dessert and coffee.

31

Sightseeing or meandering takes care of the afternoon, and journal writing. I keep awake and moving in an effort to make myself so exhausted I'll sleep through gunfire. It hasn't worked so far. Surrounded by so many different energies in a dormitory wreaks havoc with a sensitive nervous system – there are other explanations of course, but here is not the platform for launching into more esoteric doctrines.

I have the gift, a surprise of great generosity, from my Secret Agent yet I am hesitant to dip into it to take a single room in a hotel to catch up on sleep for good reasons – I don't know how long the walk will take me and I haven't yet had the inner green light for permission to abandon vestigial Camino Calvinism: *thou, Pilgrim, Shalt Suffer*. It's taken me decades to bring together the French margins of my grandmother's genes in my own personage: French, synonymous with clothes and an innate sense of colour coordination. I've been slow in redeeming the frivolity that dances in the corners of my soul and wardrobe; the yawning of severe *guilt* that accompanies the very idea of the luxury of a hotel room, *hmmmmm*, I haven't quite kicked over all the Calvin traces of a Swiss grandfather...

I can barely remember my walk to Los Arcos. It was pretty and rural. Birds sang; poppies, ox-eye daisies, honeysuckle and wild roses line the path; wheat fields young and green patchwork the distances as far the horizon; haystacks the size of apartment blocks astonish credulity. The fountains are *there* just as my water bottle needs refilling, so are the wayside milestones with their cheerful scallop shells and yellow arrows. I have my slender Michelin guide with its contour profiles and A for *albergues* at the relevant villages or towns, but one can walk without even that. I smile at the Americans and Australians with their heads in the John Brierley guide, a dreadful book, and disturbingly inaccurate at times, so heavily biased is it to JB's view of what is wholesome and good. Those who add to his considerable bank balance are walking *his* Camino, not their own: *And did you feel the Force? See the Sign? Watch the geese flying backwards? Feel the guilt when you thought an uncharitable thought?* Oh spare me the guru gabble I say to the JB brigade uncharitably and guiltlessly; sleep deprivation does nothing for my health and temper.

And at Los Arcos a snaggle toothed Austrian half my age decides, as I arrive so exhausted, I need a doctor before she'll let me in to her horrid *albergue* to rest. She takes my *mochila* from my back, turns me round, whistles for the Hound of the Baskervilles to rise from its mephitic blanket and off we march. My feeble protest: *I'm only tired, all I need is sleep,* falls on fallow ground as I register the street direction, the baker, the square, the gorgeous church and the disdain of the locals as Baskerville runs riot and pees on flower pots, doors, café table legs, the fountain. I wish I was invisible. At the clinic my prayers are answered – first, my EHIC is back in my *mochila* and second, the doctor is off for lunch. Snaggle and Baskerville abandon me. Just like that.

I make my way to the square where a sturdy Australian woman is drinking a large glass of red something with ice cubes and slices of orange. I ask her what it is. *Sangria,* she says, appraising my pilgrim lurch and rightly assessing my aches: *three of these and you'll be right,* she grins. She's right. I knock back one, and savour a second. It's nectar, pure nectar. Sitting in the square in the sunshine all's well with the world and I beam welcomes to pilgrims' as they arrive – Canadian Lovelies Gary and Tina in her Macabi and pink headband – she has her stitches out tomorrow – Australian Lovelies Vanessa and John, Austrian Ilse, Texan Colin, and three English septuagenarians who have remained in touch since school days. They live in different countries and decided to celebrate their friendship by meeting in Spain to walk the Camino.

I explore the Church. It has now opened and I am enchanted by its beauty and its Madonna. I gaze long at this Madonna, Santa Maria de los Arcos, she is lovely and steps from her twelfth century *Trône de Sagesse* to greet me *today*. I love the turn of her smile. I never confuse these images with the archetypes they represent; I gaze on them to be reminded of things eternal. I gaze on the Blessed Virgin to be reminded of *Her* parthenogenesis, a fact ignored or unknown by all but Catholics. She, too was immaculately conceived, an Immaculate Conception. Catholic 'patriarchy' didn't get it 'wrong' but every other offshoot of Christianity did. Having obliterated this mysterious continuum of the Goddess the hollow men of the Reformation dispensed with Mary and all the ancient mythos she enshrines. Today's feminists might be wiser for that knowing. My beloved Virgins in Majesty, all older than the printing press, tell me an older, richer story.

I return to Austria. It is hell on all counts. We are four women crowded in a tiny room of two, two-tiered, bunks in a room of two doors, a thoroughfare for door-slammers to reach a larger dormitory with umpteen bunks equally as crowded in the room beyond. It is a Belsen and sleepless night and almost, but not quite, the worst *albergue* I will experience. The other three women are large and each snores deafeningly. My bunk trembles. The American above me, young, pretty, very large, very privileged, her father is a consultant medical something or other and money grows on trees, is the least pleasant. She rails at all the bread she has eaten along her Camino, as if it is the only fare to be had in Spain, and when I return from my slice of bread and jam and not brilliant coffee 'breakfast' in the morning I find *my* bag of peaches and cherries and yoghurt bought for my walk has gone walkabout. So has she.

Ragged and tired and hungry after eight kilometres I stagger into Torres del Rio and by the twelve century church I almost sat down and wept. The literary allusion at least brings a smile, the plain truth is I am completely dysfunctional. I don't even know where I am headed. A woman, two women in fact, approach me and although we haven't a word of each other's language I know they know my pilgrim condition. One points me to a café; surely I understand *coffee, car, Logroño* ...? I limp over to the café and sit sipping my *café con leche* suddenly feeling extraordinarily protected. Like Jenny-any-dots I will simply, *sit*, and I take the moment to record the nightmares of the previous night in my journal as worse than a Hieronymus Bosch scene – his Monster paintings, not his Madonnas. I watch pilgrims pass, reflect on the row of Templar flags adorning the café terrace and don't care if I die right here and now since lack of sleep for days and nights has drained me of all possible life.

Fifteen minutes pass, twenty, more. The angel in the green and gold shawl from our encounter by the church wall appears, picks up my *mochila* and tells me to follow her all the way to her car, she opens the doors, puts my *mochila* in the back, closes the doors once I am in and off we drive. I don't care where we are going and sit back to enjoy the godsend, though I have the clearest sense of it being a goddess-send. Fields speed by, trails of pilgrims heading in the same direction as my angel driver seems a good sign. I acknowledge with gratitude the blessing of a walk free day wherever it is I might end up. Lanes become roads, roads grow into a freeway with switchbacks with large roundabouts and ... *Logroño*. My goodness, here I am. Pilar drops me at an *albergue* in the cobbled side street of the mediaeval centre of the town, I run round to hug her and thank her with all my heart as the *hospitalera* comes to pick up my *mochila*, invites me in and stamps my *credencial*. I feel blessed for now and when I organise myself, my bunk and my *sang-froid*, set off to explore the Cathedral, indulge in a cup of pure chocolate velvet and fall about laughing as I peer in a bookshop window to see, centre stage, a coffee-table book of – Hieronymus Bosch.

5

A Park Bench and the Witching Hour

Weather in Logroño is cold and nearly wet. I find Barclays
Bank behind arches of roses next to a building with the
prettiest decorative pargeting. I swallow my shock at the rate
of exchange, although once I am home I discover it to be
pleasantly in my favour, which just proves how dysfunctional
my brain cells. Last night was another sleepless night – but I
am wising up on rucksacks and decide that when it comes to
lugging the world on one's shoulders it seems the English
insist on cheap where Everyone Else insists on quality no
matter what cost. I discreetly lifted my bunkmate's backpack
when she went for a shower – good grief, it was *weightless*. I
noted *Gregory, Jade 35L*. *Golite Jam 35L* was another impressive
discovery. One of those weightless wonders had travelled all
the way from Le Puy. *Osprey* appealed to me no end too, all of
these happen to be American and weren't in my local
Mountain Warehouse where all the rucksacks I was shown
appeared to be made of military duty canvas. Even at double
or triple the price these super light tough nylon numbers are
worth their lightweight in gold.

A slow walk is ahead of me. I stagger up the hill into Ventosa
and a gorgeous young thing taps me on my shoulder to ask if
she may take a photo as she admires my (aged) efforts to walk
El Camino. She doesn't quite say it, but I can 'hear' it and
laugh obligingly. Her phone camera is a clever thing and she
emails it to me immediately. Ventosa is a pretty village,
population 300. Its one *albergue* is owned by an Austrian who
has registered it as a charity so she doesn't have to pay any tax,

whether because she is foreign or because of charity I don't know. Poor Spain. Cold as Charity the alburgue was too: no blankets, a centimetre of very watered down soap for use after going to the loo, cold showers because the sun, covered all day with thick dark cloud, hasn't heated the solar panels and the woman isn't putting on electricity. All this for €10 a night. There are 60 beds. She is making €600 a night and paying no tax. Wow! Breakfast is not included but there is a fridge from which one can be well ripped off. A euro for a banana, a euro for a biscuit, a euro for a tomato. Goodness me. The Austrian told me she had lived in Spain long enough to be, *More like the Spanish really*, and I can't help saying, *oh, I don't think you are like the Spanish at all*, as I think of their kindness and generosity and patience.

I return to the Bar, its name appeals, *Virgen Blanca*. A young Italian limps in, he can barely walk, his knees have given out, and a Danish woman has dreadful blisters. I'm doing alright. Then a middle-aged American couple walk in, take a table, and eat their own food without even buying a drink. They leave their peel and plastic for the staff to clean away but worse, the man removes his boots, lifts up a foot, pulls off his socks and begins picking at his blisters! On the table! I am aghast, and on behalf of all the non-English speakers present and taking up cudgels on behalf of a bar owner struggling to survive in this miniscule hamlet, (the owner is Spanish, he will pay tax) I walk over and say: *Would you behave like this in your own town? Your own country? Well, would you? These tables are for people to eat food at. Get your feet off them.*

The American looks at me blankly and grunts. And I confess to Almighty God and to you my brothers and sisters I wouldn't have patience with pilgrims who leave their manners behind when they walk through another's country. Or dare I imagine these people think it normal? I do recall cowboys films doing similar. I am enjoying giving full expression to the grumpy old woman who lives inside me and laugh at myself for having the nerve to say what others think.

My hips are seriously challenged and Everyone says my pack is too heavy for little me. The pack, not the contents. The most wondrous packs pass me, made of feather-lite fabrics. Out of these come full makeup and hairdryers not making a dint on the scales. I do have another secret though, 1000mile socks and NOK. The French and I seem to be the only pilgrims *sans* blisters. The scenery is breathtaking. Birdsong and butterflies all the way, wildflowers and sheer wonder that I am here.

I am relaxing now and walking well. I take a leaf out of the ditzy Australian's book and send my *mochila* on to my next *albergue* by Jacotrans. This is beautiful country; the hills up to Alto de San Anton are steep for me and the descent to Nájera fairly sheer. The river is fast flowing, an abundance of roses fills every garden and the fragrance of old species like Damasks and Bourbons, Louise Odier in particular, is thrilling. I so long for a garden of my own, all I can manage to grow in my estate of two square metres is a Cécile Brunner and a Ferdinand Pichard. I go into the Monasterio Santa Maria Real once I reach Nájera and find, in a deliberately darkened grotto, a fabulous Madonna. I buy a postcard and discover she is named Our Lady of the Rose. I wander the streets, find a bar offering a pilgrim meal *and* a single room for €15. Bliss. Tomorrow Santa Domingo de la Calzada.

The rain skirts my path all day. Clouds are dark, lowering, ominous, tipping down rain to my right and to my left over fields of green wheat and red poppies, a few hefty spots fall on me but the storm, which goes on and on accompanied with the wildest of buffeting winds, remains circling my path. I am so grateful and shout *thank you thank you* into the wild wind as I walk.

Goodness I feel grubby! That's okay in the fields but once I reach human habitation even the men smell lovely as they pass me, *Terre d'Hermès Eau de Toilette* apparently *de rigueur*. I shower of course, my clothes are clean if a little dusty, but I am not my usual self. I rely on flowers for fragrance, pick one each morning to tuck into the breast strap of my *mochila* or my daypack. I am now well and truly in Rioja with its soil so red and grapevines as far as the horizon. I *love* my Macabi skirt, can pee standing. Check the wind and air dry. I watch women struggle lifting huge backpacks off and on, bending and pulling down their trousers and knickers and what all and wonder what possesses women to cross-dress. I dispensed with knickers years ago convinced they were the vestigial remains of the chastity belt, a male invention. Cry Freedom!

Jacotrans takes care of my *mochila* again today, sparing the increasing pain of my hips. I will walk 15 or so miles, 21 kilometres actually, with my day pack, water, camera and journals. And I do. Santo Domingo is gorgeous, just gorgeous. I meet a lovely Frenchwoman and we share an alcove in a spartan and none too clean convent – and oh, our alcove ricochet's with the snores of twenty snorers in the main room. Christine tells me she has walked from Le Puy, she is walking to resolve her grief at the sudden death of her beloved husband to whom she was married for forty years. They walked the world together. Such sorrow fills me as she speaks. She says she knows I can feel her sadness and that I am the first person with whom she has spoken of it since she began her walk six weeks before. We sit silently on a bench in a patch of sun for a long time before going inside. She also says the only way to salvage sleep to restore one's sanity is to alternate *albergue's* with *pension* and a room of one's own.

We exchange email addresses in the morning. She is driven to walk on and I, having had another sleepless night, make the momentous decision to walk thirty metres to the *albergue* across the road and sleep. Christine laughs hugely and hugs me warmly. It is a wise decision. The five star municipal *albergue* is something else, complete with hairdryers in the spotless and superbly equipped ladies shower room. The *hospitalero* also laughs hugely as I enter at 0800 hours but he takes pity on my appearance and lets me in. They don't actually re-open until noon to allow time for cleaning. He tells me to take a top bunk in the furthest dorm, sleep while I am alone. I should have listened to Christine though, it was here the little Asian gentleman on the bunk above me practised calisthenics, shaking both bunks all night, while his mate next to me snored for Korea, or Japan, or even the whole of China. I prayed they would commit *hara kiri* and let me sleep. They bounce off their bunks at 5 am ... and the rest of us, ragged without sleep, leave too. I wondered if there is a message here for me ... something about Just Use That Gift and Get a Life!

Heavenly walk in mist and rain, the Dawn Chorus amplified. Recall that John Brierley called this particular stretch of road "soulless". As a man is so he sees. It is shimmeringly alive with winged singers – birds, dearest *souls*. Ah well, as the Sufi says: in a room full of saints a thief will only see pockets. John Brierley sees soulless – says much of him. A friend gave me JB's guide when I first decided to walk, so glad I read it then, choked on his sanctimonious pap and abandoned it.

I reflect on things as I walk. Leaving early I sock and NOK my feet, put a small pull of M's gift of Blue Leicester fleece between my little toes and rubbed L's gift of Thai balm into my thighs to warm the muscles. I send up silent thanks to all. A beautiful walk, wild and windy and sleeting rain all around me again. I carry Caroline's poncho and fight ferocious elements to engulf myself in it with help from Nadine and André passing from Pas de Calais; they began their walk in Le Puy. I pass Belgian Denis on his *return* from Santiago – he has notched up *5240 kilometres*, obviously via Montenegro.

Double rainbows arch over El Camino as I walk spritely into the first town for coffee and brioche. I'm only going to Viloria de Rioja today, but leaving at 5 am means I arrive hours too early for the *albergue* to open so I sit freezing on the stone step, clothed in everything I've brought and wrapped in my poncho as a wind break. The pitfall of sending the *mochila* ahead is that I can't retrieve it from behind the very locked doors to continue walking if I arrive early. Big Mistake. Knocking on the door has no response, indeed there is a sign saying: *do not knock before 13.30.* I sit on the freezing stone step to watch the storm circle me. The village has no bar, no café, no shelter. I forget it is Sunday and foolishly haven't planned for provisions to get me through the noonday blood sugar crunch.

I leave the freezing stone step of the *albergue* door and go to perch on a wooden bench at the side of the *albergue* from where I can see pilgrims passing on the street up there on the rise. Two men sit on the park bench. In broad familiar accents one says to the other: *gees, look it that old Sheila down there on that bench, doesn't she look a witch.* His mate agrees wholeheartedly.

I am astonished. They mean *me*. I deliberate on whether to call out and congratulate their perspicacity but resist the temptation. I know they are using the word for wise woman in its most pejorative way but I do wrestle with my urge to respond in Australian: *youse guys've got it right fer once, a good hex'll sort youse out for the rest of yer walk*, but I know the tincture of embarrassment of being understood, and the irony, will be lost on them.

My mood drops as my blood sugar hits Low and darkens as storm clouds close in around me like the Four Horsemen of the Apocalypse. When the two old Australian witch hunters have left I move up to the wooden park bench on the main street thinking it warmer than the stone step and the wet wooden tree trunk I am alternately warming. I wonder how I will get through the next hours. A Dutch couple are about to pass when the man asks why I am sitting here and I manage to grumble through the dark clouds of my mind: *I'm waiting for a miracle. I need food.*

Food? he replies, *you need food?* I *have food*, and he sits down beside me and produces biscuits and cheese and the woman sits on the other side of me and produces a knife and bread and chorizo and chocolate and as I eat my own dark clouds lift and I am back to normal. Even the Four Horsemen hover without menace. A van pulls up and out jumps a local man with bottles of water to give us because we are *peregrinos*. Oh people are so kind. The Dutchman bids the Dutchwoman walk on; they are not a couple, he says he wants to tell me his story.

Rewind: Glastonbury 12th May 2014
The day before I left Glastonbury for my Camino a Dutch friend came to see me and to give me a gift for my pilgrimage. Johanna knew about walking. She had walked from Le Hague to Jerusalem, 5000 kilometres, 3500 miles. She went through all the countries on a straight line on the map from Holland to Israel – that's a lot of countries – carrying her rucksack, a tent, her flute and her eyeliner. She said I ought to go to Finisterre after reaching Santiago, and this gift was to be a reminder. She held out to me a large and beautiful medallion of Our Lady of Finisterre. I accepted it and wear it pinned with a large gold safety pin on the inside of one of the deep pockets of my skirt. I left home to walk the Camino on 13th May 2014.

Karel begins his story: *On 12th May 2010 my daughter Linda and my son in law Jeffrey died on their honeymoon in an air crash. No one survived the crash. On 13th May 2014 I left home to walk the Camino. The day before was the Memorial Day of the disaster. On that day the closest girlfriend of my daughter gave me a small stone heart and said she had put one like it on the grave of Linda and Jeffrey.* "Take this heart with you and Linda's and your heart will be connected on your journey."

I am looking for a miracle, said Karel, tears filling his eyes, *my daughter and I had a very close relationship. The year before the air disaster she wrote a poem of our special father daughter relationship which gave us so much joy. She said she wanted to share the joy with the world so she put her poem into a bottle and we went to the pier at Scheveningen where she threw the bottle into the sea. I am going to walk to Finisterre because I am looking for a miracle. My prayer to my heavenly Father is that the bottle with the message that my daughter threw into the sea the year before she died will be washed ashore in Finisterre when I am sitting on the beach at the end of my Camino.*

As Karel unfolds his heartaching story I can barely contain such sorrow. I know what I must do. *Karel,* my voice slow with the weight of sadness, *God always gives us miracles but,* my voice slows even more*, sometimes the miracles don't quite come in the way we hope for. On 12th May a Dutch friend who lives in my town came to say goodbye and to give me a gift. She had walked from Le Hague to Jerusalem and her book is published in Dutch. She said I must walk to Finisterre and she gave to me a medallion which would protect me on my Way.*

I was fiddling in my pocket, unpinning Our Lady of Finisterre. I brought it out, holding it in the palm of my hand: *I believe this is meant for you to have; your daughter is always with you.*

Sometimes a mystery is too overpowering and one can sense the Presence of the Unseen worlds. The Silence then surrounding us stilled the attention of the whole natural world – the wind had stopped, no pilgrims passed by us, the birds had ceased to sing – and in this holy moment Karel's daughter Linda was intimately close. Karel accepted the gift. The guiding synchronicities of our journeys that led to our meeting *now* are clear. I had to be hungry, I had to wait for the *albergue* to open.

We hug. Karel takes a 'selfie' of us as he goes on his way, waving and singing a song he had learned for the Camino. I go down to the *albergue* which is about to open. My day of Moments hasn't ended. Acacio, the *albergue* owner, chides me for not pre-booking. He then tells me he was fully booked yesterday and is fully booked tomorrow, but tonight there is one bed available. He lets me use his personal computer and because it is a personal computer and not a public one microsoft allow me access to my emails. It will be the last time I am able to. I find an email from Olivia in America which begins:

Dearest
I am walking the Camino with you in spirit as I read Paulo Coelho's The Pilgrimage ....

I look up at the wall above me. There is a life sized photo of Paul Coelho. *Acacio*, I ask, *why is there a portrait of Paulo Coelho looking at me?* And I am beyond being astonished when I hear something along the lines of: *I am from Brazil, I know Paulo Coelho and he is the Patron, the Godfather, of this albergue..*

Dearest Olivia
    You won't believe this but I am replying to your email as I sit under a portrait of Paulo Coelho who happens to be Patron of this albergue

Here in this tiny *albergue* of nine beds I meet Ela and Christina from Canada, Jüergen from Austria, Celso a cyclist from Brazil and Simone from Belgium. Simone and I roast our socks over the fire to dry. It is cold here. I learn that Simone is 81 and has feet so deformed by bunions she can only walk in socks and sandals. She will walk the whole Camino. I will meet her again.

44

6

Saint John of the Nettles, Roses and Rosemary

During the evening meal, under the watchful gaze of Paulo Coelho, mine host, Acacio, tells me I should write a book on aging and women and walking the Camino. He says the research I did in preparation is impressive. Celso, the Brazilian, looks at my *mochila* and pronounces it 'military' and too heavy by half. Jüergen has shin splints and walks slowly, limiting himself to 15 kilometres or so for now.

In the morning warm goodbyes are said and we head off into the wind. The rule at this *albergue* states no one is to rise before 7 am. Very civilized. My day's walk is a joy. I pass through Grañón, pause at the bakery of Jesus where hot *bollitos* are just being drawn from the oven and the fragrance of fresh bread fills the lonely street.

I talk to everything as I walk, tell everything how perfect it is – puddles, wind, flowers, grasses, birds, lizards, trees – they understand and I am flooded with love. The Way walks me. It's as if I am awakening to a dual consciousness. I will still rail at the snorers or whatever else irritates my human frailty, but there is another, deeper, reality which takes over the minute I step onto the true Way and am surrounded by nature. I'm walking well, the land is singing. I am overcome by a profound love for my dear feet and plump body, almost apologising to them for embarking on such a reckless adventure at their age. I love the newness of feeling body-me respond to the superhuman, and seemingly impossible task, of walking 500 miles *in my own body*! I don't always live there. My good humour returns apace and I smile as I enter the marvellous town of Belorado, many kilometres further on, to stand staring in wonder at the extraordinary sight of storks nesting in colossal and precariously perched nests built on every ledge of the church bell tower.

After admiring the church I continue on to the tiny hamlet of Villambistia where I am greeted by the singularly attractive woman *hospitalera* of San Roque. San Roque, so well loved in the south of France where he is particularly associated with Mary Magdalene for some reason that escapes me now; a good place to stop. I choose my bunk, but the dorm fills up quickly. *No, I don't snore*, says a singularly unaware elderly man from somewhere south of Arlington when I ask him so as I can position myself as far away as possible. Above me is Jüergen. We decide we like each other's company as bunkmates as we agree that we are such quiet sleepers. Jüergen is still suffering from shin splints. I go for a walk and find a deep cerise damask rose and some sprigs of rosemary. I bring these back to the dorm where he is resting. He is awake. I give him the rose and the rosemary and say he must sleep with these on his pillow and breath in their fragrance visualizing it flow all the way down to his injuries and: *it will heal the pain,* he grins, entering into the play I am inventing as the only way I can offer my sympathy. He gets it, he really *gets* it.

The worst night of snoring, according to Jüergen, came from the American from south of Arlington who said he didn't snore. He snored and rattled and belched and threw himself about the bed – sheer hell for us all. There is always *one*.

Few of us slept. An Aboriginal woman from Sydney's inner city mutters darkly but nothing short of pointing the bone would have penetrated that man's blissful sleep. None of us happened to have a spare metacarpal handy. It was still dark when we, the sleep ravaged, called it a night and left before murder. Yet, there's a crack in everything, that's how the light gets in, and once again, the moment I am beyond the village and on the Camino, love floods through me as the birds tune up for their Dawn Chorus, the pink and gold clouds stream light above the village which appears cast in molten flames. No one speaks as we each walk into the morning.

Up to the peaks through the fragrant pine forests I walk, not the dead pine forests we know but pine forests alive with siskins, red squirrels, crossbills and lizards and much more besides. Over the Rio Cerrata, down into San Juan de Ortega and down down down into Agés. I rest alone at San Juan, feeling suddenly shy and slightly ill at ease with the bonhomie of so many pilgrims. Their chatter prevents much interaction with the world around them so when an emerald lizard freezes as everyone passes it by I am enthralled when it relaxes and sits as I take photos before it vanishes into the bracken with a quick flick of his tail. The church is light filled, empty of all but its story: in folklore here bees are unborn souls; San Juan de Ortega – St John of the Nettles – is buried here and when his tomb was opened in the fifteenth century white bees with fragrant odour rose from his tomb. I recall that the first temple of Delphi was built of bees wings, and that I once read of a species of bee which slows its wingbeat to the note of middle C in order to activate the release of pollen.

I walk twenty one kilometres happily, and reach Agés by two o'clock. The first *albergue* is San Rafael; I so enjoy the company of saints that I stop right here. A wildly eccentric *hospitalero*, who refuses to be photographed, wags his finger at me for not booking beforehand (all the good guides say you can't book refugios, but maybe that is arbitrary) but leads me upstairs to a charming room of two by two bunks with pretty blue and white floral duvets, thick pillows, white sheets, a huge walk in wardrobe, ensuite shower and loo and views over the fields. Was it 8€ or 10€? Whatever, it was worth it. A woman comes in, asks where I am from. *Glastonbury!* she exclaims, *I must phone my husband, he is there now, passionate about King Arthur!* Before she phones I hold up my Glastonbury Spring water bottle for her to photograph the label of the Tor which she texts to him. These modern phones are really clever. I think she called it Smart. It is a giggle. Amalia is an architect from Venezuela. I go downstairs to eat and when I return to my room on the pillow of the bunk above me there is a cerise rose and two sprigs of rosemary. Jüergen! He comes in grinning, *I knew it was you* he says, *I see your hat and your red and white polka dot ribbon!* We are in for a quiet night with just the three of us. Wonderful.

Amalia has left at first light, silently, and I silently leave next. Jüergen is sleeping with the rose on his pillow. He will walk faster today, miraculously his shin splints have healed. He continues to carry the rose and rosemary attached to the top of his rucksack. I am rather touched but know that he will now travel far ahead of me. Encounters like this, short and meaningful, make up my amalgam of memories.

Today it rains. And rains. I stop for breakfast in Atapueca, a village famous for unearthing stone aged hominids dating back 400,000 years, the oldest in Western Europe. Matagrande looms ahead, nearly 1200 metres. This climb it is really difficult, the rain has made the rocky ascent glacially slippery and we pilgrims pick our way footfall by tenuous footfall. Dry, it may be alright, but wet is hazardous. We trail like ants, slowly and separately, the sense of deep concentration palpable. I don't know how I reach the top, but I do, just as another lone pilgrim is passing the huge cross in the mist. I stop momentarily, take a photo in the rain, aware that the yellow shrub at the foot of the Cross is the only patch of light and colour in this dark and haunting place.

Thankful I am to leave it. The descent is not so difficult. Ahead of me I see one pilgrim walking slowly, painfully and saturated. It is Simone. We greet and part, her poor ill-formed feet are soaked in their sandals. I am headed for Burgos 20 kilometres ahead and still many hours walk. The rain is relentless.

Burgos. Exhausted, I find the tiny *albergue* that John Brierley found so appealing. Big Mistake. He is such hypocrite, he stays at paradors, *paradors* I ask you, at no less than 200€ a night, and recommends this pitiful place. It is parochial; perhaps he thinks parochial is synonymous with 'spiritual'. The *hospitaleros* are kind, most are, but that doesn't make it 'spiritual'. The *albergue* is rich with intention but horribly poor with what wet tired pilgrims need. First I climb the many stairs winding up a narrow stairwell to come to a crowded room above a pretty church. Alas one shower and one functional loo for eighteen people just won't do. The hot water has gone, the loo is occupied.

I am offered a top bunk which I cannot climb up to. A young American athlete has the last lower one. I insist on swapping. In my tiredness the noise and proximity of people flips me over to a more than mild insanity and I stand in confusion lost under the armpits of six huge male Californian bullet-proof sophomores on a holiday jaunt to Santiago. I vaguely register that these privileged (or they wouldn't be attending university) young men are here because it is *donativo*, 5€. In the same instant I am aware that Simone has also staggered up the three flights of stairs and has been told there is no bed. Not one, not *one* of the healthy young things offer their bed to this crippled, wet, 81 year woman. So far below their armpits stood she that they don't even see her. In a nanosecond I reach over and say there *is* a bed, take mine. The *hospitalero* looks at me with such grace, and Simone, removing her dripping poncho, put her arms round me to say in halting English: *God has sent you to me, thank you, I can walk no more.* Meanwhile the armpits and elbows above us try to shuffle about to give an inch of floor space for Simone's *mochila*. I wearily pick up mine and head down the flights of narrow stairs and out into the wet streets, chilled to the bone, soaking wet and lost, to look for somewhere to lay my own head.

7

Burgos, Brollies and Polka Dots

Burgos was so cold and the rain so heavy it penetrated my poncho. When Simone had removed hers to hug me she was also dripping wet underneath it – two dripping dames. Our ponchos are well respected brands intended for poor weather, but not Camino weather apparently. I trudge on along the street at a trajectory from the vast Cathedral, only dimly aware of the attractive shops to the left and right of me. Where am I to go? I don't know. I am numb with tiredness and cold. Reaching the end of the pedestrian way I see with a sense of gratitude the scallop shells set into the centre of the cobbled road. I have met up with the Camino again. I look around me. Goodness me, there is El Cid! And on my right is a rather grand hotel façade with a proud few stars under its name: *Norte y Londres*. My goodness, I draw breath, I was *born* in north London way back in Dreamtime; this must be a Sign.

I sigh, to give myself a sense of courage, and take my dripping pilgrim-worn self into the chandeliered and sparkling foyer. The receptionist of this oldest posada on this Camino doesn't bat an eye at the dripping scarecrow in front of her and I find myself asking if there is a room, for two nights. There is. Top floor, double room, single *peregrina* price of 40€ per night. I've done it, cracked the Calvinist. And there is a *bath*, and thick white towels to dry with. I peel off my sopping clothes, string up my trusty washing line across the windows and support it by looping the cord over the hinges of the open windows. The rain doesn't come in as the windows, being on the top floor, are well under the eaves. I hang everything. The poncho

I throw over the shower rail once I've had a long, hot, sublime soak in the bath. I am a new woman now and dress in my other skirt, other top, dry socks and sandals. Socks and sandals. I cringe that I could ever have walked the streets of this elegant city wearing *socks* and *sandals*. But my boots are wet and my hotel room is warm, heated by central heating – it is important that everything I have will dry properly.

Dodging and dashing between covered colonnades the monsoonal rain drives me to enter a bespoke umbrella shop; I go inside and covet two. I have to remind myself that back in Glastonbury I have a collection of umbrellas that stop traffic; once, a woman tapped me on my shoulder as I walked passed the Clock Tower in Tref-y-Clawdd one wet day and said that particular umbrella was worth mugging for. I have Valentinos' and Florentino's; a Pierre Cardin with pearl raindrops sewn all over; a Ruby and Ed with frills; a My Fair Lady Ascot stripe in black and white; an umbrella decorated with a wet Parisian street scene bought from a street vendor on a similarly wet day in Paris and a Parisian vintage with a double layer and ebony handle circa 1951 given to me by Greek friend who lived in Paris then. I have micro brollies in handbags and micro brollies in the car, an Alfa Romeo brolly that almost covers a pond – I do brollies *really* well. I do not need another brolly, no matter how monsoonal the weather today, or tomorrow for that matter, I will curl up in my warm room and have three hot baths instead.

First, food. From an organic delicatessen along from the bespoke umbrella shop I buy slices of Serrano hams, artisan bread, water, Tarta de Queso. Round a corner I come upon an entire shop of organic yoghurts from every region of Spain and from every source of milk – ewe, cow, nanny goat. I am dazzled by the selection with their stamps and seals of authenticity but dazzled doesn't deter me from buying one too many. Then to a greengrocer for sweet white-fleshed remarkably juicy peaches, luscious ripe tomatoes and, hurrah, a Lebanese cucumber. This is the one vegetable I miss from life in Australia – their flavour, their non-acidity, their fine skin and their small size makes them perfect for halving length-wise, sprinkling with a touch of pure sea salt, Guérande or Gozo, letting the salt rest on the flesh for a while and then eating them just as they are. Delish.

Now I need a hot three course pilgrim meal to set me up for hibernating for a couple of days with picnics until the rain stops. I find a tiny family restaurant off the main pedestrian way and am served by the portly owner with food cooked by his mother. Seeing my pilgrim status the owner plumps a photo album of his own Caminos' down on my table to look at. He had walked all four, criss-crossing Spain a mere four years ago. Manolo's considerable girth is hugely encouraging for I must be the only *peregrina* to be putting *on* weight from all the amazing food.

Full fed and calm again, laden with all my delicious purchases, I walk back to London, mostly protected by shop awnings and the canopy of other umbrellas. Life size street sculpture in this rather grand city is impressive; I love the young woman walking out under *her* umbrella. Rain must be a given here. A *peregrina* from Cairns told me she had carried a pink umbrella when she walked her Camino. How gorgeous! I pass an accessory shop and pop in to look for eyeliner, none there, but to my surprise and delight I find a red and white polka dot Alice band. I laugh at the image of me wearing it as I walk into Santiago – and buy it, just in case. There it is, with its mirror mnemonic on my rucksack which causes much mirth, especially on my boots which are often photographed by other pilgrims. When I've taken its photo I notice that my bed cover is also red with tiny white dots. Laughter re-activates my endorfuns which in turn brings me the best night: holy sleep, holy solitude. A cosy bed with white soft cotton sheets, under a thick camel coloured merino wool blanket, a warm room and the bliss of ... holy *silence*.

It is still raining hard the next morning but I am staying two nights, and for sure the weather will clear on the third day. Things happen in threes. I read the room brochures. The hotel was founded in 1904, is "dean of the City" and the oldest of all the Posadas del Camino de Santiago. Well, well, what a blessing I have been led too, and I send up a prayer that Simone slept well too.

There are a couple of times through my second day when the torrential downpours lessen enough to give me a sort of dry run to the Cathedral, a building of staggering scale and intricacy containing splendid artwork. But having reached it, and wandered about its shop and entrance, I simply can't bring myself to go in. I want to explore the old city walls and great ascending steps to the castle built by Alfonso X, Alfonso *el Sabio*, who commissioned Catholics, Muslims and Jews to his Court to compose music, hymns and *cantigas* to the Virgin Mary. Spain during the 13th century, when King Alfonso reigned, was, like him, wise. It was also home to Islam and Mary in Islam holds as much weight as in Catholicism. I learned this during my long pilgrimage along the Old Silk Road during the 1980's when I became enamoured of a Kurd, the Kurds and Kurdistan, a combination which greatly broadened my education in theology, geography, politics and ... kilims. My Camino pilgrimage, though I can't articulate even to myself why I am doing it, inclines me to reflect on those deeper verities that were once embedded in the soil and soul of Spain.

The views of the Cathedral from high above the city are splendid, worth my long climb. The rain catches me out once I leave the shelter of the forest but I have the hot bath to look forward to for comfort and don't much mind. A nun leaving the St Vincent de Paul hostel blows me a kiss as she trots off down long flights of steps to the lower part of the city. I love the old centre of Burgos around the environs of its Cathedral and I venture across the river to the Museums and Art

Galleries, small churches, street sculptures, river walks, elegant people and special shops and spent every hour exploring and visiting much that is here. Tomorrow my footprints here will be blown away with the wind; though never seen they will remain like ghostly imprints of all the *peregrinos* who have set their step to Santiago for over a thousand years. The thought is wholly nourishing. I love my feet.

And on the third day when I look out of the window there is enough blue sky to make a pair of sailor's trousers – the rain is passing.

8

The Hospital of the Soul

06.06 a.m. I leave North London. It is difficult to leave such comfort but exciting to be on the Way again for now will begin days of walking the Meseta all the way to León and the very thought is thrilling. The Meseta evokes strong reactions – some hate it, some think it too boring to walk and take buses to avoid it, others are passionate about the contemplative impact of four days walking across the endless high tablelands of wheat with little to distract their thoughts. An Australian songwriter friend said of his crossing the Meseta that he was taking his life for a walk, used the time as an interior résumé.

I had never walked much in Australia, its open bush didn't invite intimate exploration for a lone woman and *refugios* hadn't taken route along the droving trails. However, its vast skies and open horizons always sent my pulse racing. An ancient remembrance of the nomad buried deep in my soul burned inside me, a response to walking as a way of life. Hermit? Monk? Sannyasa? Peregrina? Who would know.

I fill up my water bottle, tie my food in a plastic bag and loop it over the waist straps of my *mochila*, NOK and 1000mile sock my feet, roll up my poncho and walk out into the dawn light. At the edge of the city the cockleshells appear to stop I stand to ponder which direction to take. It is early, nothing is open, no one is about to ask, nothing is open. Two teenagers with school packs are hurrying in the opposite direction on the opposite side of the wide road, I call to ask the way. They've never heard of the Camino. Taken aback I acknowledge to myself that this is a huge city and why would young ones, or anyone for that matter, when the excitement of the present and future is all around them, bother themselves with a path from the mediaeval past which daft people choose to walk.

Quelling the rising anxiousness, I ponder where to go, my sense of direction doesn't feel right from where I am standing. I hesitate, turn around, walk back aways. A man appears, I ask him, he is in a hurry, indicates I should follow him. Down and through old lanes and small alleys we go, he is surely hurrying and I find it hard to keep up with my *mochila* on my back. He barely stops at a street corner but turns: *passo del Río*, he calls, indicating with hand gestures I must turn right once I am over the bridge. Gathering courage I cross the river and turn right. Here the cockleshells are clear, the road is wide avenue'd and tree'd, a grand statue of a king as a pilgrim confirms my inner comfort that I am back on the Way. The cockleshells are clearly marked, sparkle in the puddles around them from the recent rain. I breathe easily.

Actually the smaller scallop shells, one of which I have on my *mochila*, *is* a true cockleshell and the Magna Carta grants every citizen of the British Isles the right to collect up to eight pounds of cockles from the foreshore for him or herself. Above that amount is deemed commercial fishing. I walk alone for a couple of hours, no rain, wondrously cool. Once I reach the open fields the sun is beginning to edge the trees gold, pilgrims pass me, the Italians and French call *buen Camino* as they pass, the Germans and Australians don't. It is almost a vocal talisman, *buen Camino,* a blessing to a fellow pilgrim from long ago when the Way was fraught with dangers and difficulties – few hot baths in those days – and a deeply rooted courtesy. Keenly, I register the discourtesy of *not* wishing fellow pilgrims well. And rue the loss of good manners. *Buen Camino* has a special charm and power when offered by a stranger.

As I am walking through a gloomy tunnel I hear voices behind me. The tunnel amplifies them, they are shouting and the echo distorts them and I hurry out of the tunnel to the open field. Laughing, John catches up with me, Vanessa is not far behind. I am thrilled to see them and we fall in step. As we walk a Frenchman walks past with a marvellous wheeled chariot attached to his hips. I am astonished and ask him about it, Yves is happy to stop to tell me all about his wondrous *randonée* chariot made in Lille. I take photos, make notes. I am seriously impressed.

Tardajos is a small village ten kilometres or so beyond Burgos, the world of pilgrims seems to have gathered here for coffee and *el desayuno*. John and Vanessa have sad tales to tell of the *albergue* where I had given my bunk to Simone. They had a top and a bottom bunk. In the morning Vanessa picked up her *mochila* and was on her way to the landing and stairs as John was climbing down from the top bunk. He had already swung his daypack down to the lower bunk as Vanessa was leaving. When he reached the floor and turned to collect the daypack, in that split second, his daypack had gone. Taken off guard he thought Vanessa had taken it as she had left, so, hurriedly putting on his own *mochila*, he caught up with her on the stairs. Alas, she hadn't picked it up. Worse was the loss of his camera, a top of the range Sony DSLR, in the bottom of his daypack. With it went its memory card and hundreds of photos. Their stay there was made worse, he said, by the arrival of a group of older NZ women who had bussed it all the way from somewhere and were standing in the registration queue almost adjacent to the bunks. One of their kind was refusing to pay the *hospitalero* the paltry *donativo* of 5€. Poor Spain.

A familiar smile greets us as we eat breakfast – Amalia from way back in Agés. Her story adds to the grim tales from Burgos. She was having lunch in a bar on her first day, her *mochila* safely stowed under her table, but when she had finished her meal and had bent to retrieve it, it had vanished. The entire *mochila* had been spirited away from under her very nose. She had to replace absolutely everything. It cost her dear in days, the city is large, what she needed was out in the satellite shopping centres. Lucky she speaks Spanish.

Across the road we watch a French *peregrino* and his donkey pass by. Man and donkey walk side by side, have come from somewhere beyond the Pyrénées. These French! They are *so* inventive. The Way calls, we lift our *mochilas* and take to the road.

Vanessa has pulled a tendon and we walk slowly together, further on the three of us picnic on my poncho. It is a pretty walk, wheatfields and poppies, corn cockles and cornflowers line the path. We reach Hornillos del Camino and neither Vanessa or I can walk another step. I have walked 20 kilometres to Hornillos del Camino with my full pack. I am suitably amazed with myself. Vanessa takes a couple of my heavy duty Ibuprofen and when the pain in her leg has gone she heroically sets off to find a private Casa Rural as the only *albergue* was full. The Casa is a splendid new house built by two generations, the third generation is three months old and winning over all who coo at his gurgling smile. Our room is large, heated, three new beds covered with thick duvets and luxurious satin counterpanes, ensuite and we have the use of an extremely well-stocked kitchen and fridge. The young couple's generosity is touching, we are almost the first guests of their brave new venture and while we all know pilgrims are a ready income many walkers can be selfish, demanding and disrespectful. I would love to think the kindness of this family is never abused, their golden generosity never tarnished.

Vanessa is fairly bouncing after the Ibuprofen and cooks a superb pasta filled with all manner of good things. She invites a stray Norwegian to join us; the woman has a stentorian voice and finds herself highly amusing. She doesn't pause for breath after speaking but rocks herself into an insane laughter before taking up the previous thread and continuing her confused anecdotes at a volume of decibels just short of an invitation to murder. She is oblivious to any hint that John, Vanessa or I just *may* have a word or two to say ourselves. I eat and excuse myself to return upstairs to the silence of our room. I carry guilt with me, I shirked the washing up.

Today is the second day of walking the Meseta and we are off to Castrojeriz, 20 kilometres ahead of us. It is a magical path and the weather is kind. At an uncommonly cool 10 degrees C, a slight breeze, lowering clouds, a *chiaroscuro* of dancing light and shade as the wind jostles clouds across the sun it is the perfect gift for a day's walk. We all leave at the same time but soon separate as we find our own pace. I pass a man on crutches, hospital crutches, but he has a *mochila* on his back so he probably intends walking the Camino. A rainbow arcs across the sky right over him. Ahead a plump young woman wearing star spangled black leggings smiles happily as I pass her and tell her how lovely they are. Poppies, growing in profusion, pose in perfection; birdsong, similar to the Australian coastal pardalote follows me. I stand for a long time trying to see the source of this surprising sound as I know it is definitely not a pardalote, but even as it accompanies me I am unable to catch sight of it in the thick waving wheat. A *frisson* of nostalgia ripples like the wind in the wheat across my storehouse of pardalote memories: I would spend hours watching these tiny birds burrow nests in the coastal sand dunes at the foot of my garden near the Kingscliff coast forty years ago.

We walk into Hontanas as the church clock strikes ten, spend a moment or two photographing the shrine of St Bridget. I completely forgot, if I ever knew, that she and her husband went on pilgrimage to Santiago de Compostela in the 14th century. When they returned to Sweden her husband died and she became known for her works of charity, particularly toward unwed mothers and their children. Birgitta became a member of the Third Order of St Francis and devoted herself to prayer and care for the poor and the sick. I stayed with the Brigidine Sisters of her religious foundation last Christmas when I went to Assisi.

In the main square of this hamlet a surprise – Ela and Christina, last seen with Paulo Coelho. I introduced all these Lovelies to each other and they warn us to bypass the first café, their coffee was lukewarm. They had spent a miserable night in the Hornillos *albergue* that we had, to our good fortune, found full. The second and the third bars in the village are closed but from the last drifts a divine smell of food. We forget the coffee and have hot fresh chicken soup for the soul and buy *pan du chocolate* straight from the oven to take with us for picnics. As we sit there John, ruing the loss of his camera, tells us that in the Middle Ages there had been a Papal Bull stating that pilgrims who steal from pilgrims will burn in hell. A most restorative thought. The Jacotrans driver comes in with *mochilas* for the *albergue*, he notices my walking stick, recognises its menomic of red and white polka dots, smiles and says: "your *mochila* is safe with me", and drives away to deliver it to Castrojeriz.

We pause to explore the atmospheric ruined Abbey of San Anton along the way, niches of little Santiago statues and remnants of Tau crosses lend a special sense of being surrounded by Presences, and not quite as alone as we thought we were. The great doorway holds significance for early pilgrims and alms of food would be given them as they passed on to Castrojeriz with its single street of three kilometres. Three kilometres, that's half way to the next village. We take a room for three at the *Albergue* de Peregrinos, a splendidly restored barn and mill that also offers a pilgrim meal. We shower, refresh and go to explore. John and I walk to the end of the village, and prove what happens when one walks and talks in two's or three's or more – we miss the essentials. On the return walk – can I imagine adding all these extra kilometres to a walk of what will be for me, with detours, 500 miles, I must be daft – we meet Vanessa who excitedly tells us of an enchanting encounter at the Hospital of the Soul. John and I, talking, had walked right passed it.

Hospital del Alma, a house with no doors. How could I have missed it? It is a miracle. Mau and Nia met some years ago on the Camino and eventually they settled here and opened not only their extraordinary home, a creative renovation in process, but the generosity of their creative selves and their love for the Camino to all who are led to enter the open front door. There is a front door, only. Mau said so many doors had closed in his life he wanted to live only with open spaces under the lintels. We were invited to wander at leisure, encouraged to explore upstairs and down, to help ourselves to the cakes and teas and fruit spread out on the rough hewn table. Their home is filled with curiosities, cottage antiques, salvaged charms of painted and decorated panels, fabrics, textures, flowers, herbs, fragrance: rose petals in bowls of water, incense, holy silence, a photographic exhibition. Paths, paved, cobbled, sgraffito'd, led around the garden to the caves at the back where Mau and Nia have built the Wild Chapel, placed the Laughing Cross.

The Camino, said Nia, whose beauty holds me spellbound, *is not done with our feet, but our Life.* She and Mau spoke of chasing shadows, those ephemeral will o' the wisps named success, fame, fortune. Success, fame and fortune have certainly all escaped me. Being in the presence of Nia and Mau I feel a sense of being enriched in my *own* presence. I used to feel that in the presence of my friend Bahli when she was alive; she too would give meaning to the tessarae of my own fragmented existence, an existence which gives me grave cause for concern at times. I look back over emptiness and a few colourful dots. Bahli said those few colourful dots of mine were what gave her faith in her own journey.

After such blessings I spend a sleepless night – it is about now that I learn microsoft has blocked access to my email so thoroughly I am unlikely to ever contact my world of friends ever again. John has tried every which way unsuccessfully to access it through his laptop. I lay fretting and counteracting my thoughts, fretting and counteracting them with positive alternatives the whole night through. I am so *cross* with microsoft, how *can* they do this, I argue to myself, to a nearly 70 year woman walking alone 500 miles across northern Spain, in a country whose language she doesn't know? Would the nerd who blocked it do this to his *mother*, his *grandmother?* I fume. I know I have to *really* stress now so I can let the whole scenario go tomorrow – which is another day. It works. In the morning I can rise, dress and pronounce – *well, that's it then, I'm free to walk without bothering about blogs, friends, or anything else.* I wonder if my long silence might prematurely invite the Requiem Mass I'd left with Father James, but I sent the thought packing. So what if it does – Resurrection's not new.

9

The Road Less Travelled

It is a very long climb up to Alto de Mostelares, nearly 1000 metres, over the river and out of Castrojeriz (population 853, I note) and down down a steep descent to 350 metres and a Y decision. At the high point two more crosses mark the deaths of two pilgrims, I wonder what they died of. The dates show them to be decades younger than me. We come to a fork in the road with two signs, one faded pointing straight on and one, much newer and more prominent, pointing to the left. A Frenchman, with whom we had dined last night in Castrojeriz, prominent in a cheery red jacket, is sitting in the wheat by the straight track. My feet turn themselves to this track, dotted on the sign, which points to Itero del Castillo. Every other pilgrim takes the Camino trail left without so much as a glance at this other possibility. A *frisson* of hesitation makes me pause – I could be wrong about this. Vanessa follows me, calls to John who is fast disappearing left along the main Camino track. He climbs bank up the bank to join us, swears he will throttle me if ...

We walk the track in silence. Underfoot is soft and dry rather like powder, gentle on the feet. Far to my left on a pitiless stretch of very empty road I see dots of pilgrims walking under the sun. Today isn't hot, lucky for us all. After a pretty but Very Long Walk we come to a tiny, rather desolate, hamlet with a vast square tower high above the houses, an attractive standing stone and cross, a *fuente* and a church – but no bar, no café, no shop. Things are looking bleak, we have been walking many hours and need breakfast. I am not looking forward to being throttled…

Exactly as I reach the last house in the village the front door springs open and a handsome man with the manners and elegance of a Spanish *grandee* appears. He smiles at us and I ask if he knows of a bar or café where we might have coffee. He looks, well, slightly concerned I think, as if he doesn't want to burden such a lovely morning with bad news – there is no bar in Itero del Castillo; in fact there are no longer any pilgrims passing through Itero del Castillo because there is no longer any bridge linking Itero del Castillo with Itero de la Vega – it was washed away years ago. But he holds all this to himself for the time being and calls up to the upper window where appears his attractive wife. A few words exchanged and: *you are welcome in our home for coffee*, he smiles, looking back at us.

What a delightful home it is. Lovingly restored, fascinating old pieces everywhere, a landing whose floor has been removed to reveal the charming parlour below, that room is adjacent to the room we are led to. And the bathroom – oh so pretty and filled with exquisitely embroidered linens, small towels of drawn threadwork and old hand lace curtains.

We spend two, or is it three, memorable hours with Fernando and Rosa, reluctant to leave this charming interlude of elegant and cultured company, good coffee, toast, butter, apricot jam and their last three almond biscuits. Today is their day to shop and stock up. Vanessa brings out her phone to share photos of her grandchildren with Rosa, who shares her own. Their womanly pleasure is delightful to see. Fernando is a retired lecturer in agriculture, cereals, as I understand it, from the University of Valladolid. The name launches me into the remarkable account of my obtaining a Spanish *credencial* from Valladolid before I even set foot in Spain and drew many questions from the two of them of the Glastonbury legends and the church of St Mary which conversation then leads on to Philip of Spain and the writing on the wall for English Catholics during the horrors of the Reformation in the 1530's. This led to the invitation of Philip in 1538 to found an English seminary in Valladolid – the point in question. *Ah,* smiles Fernando, *this Camino is your holy camino* and I respond: *and meeting you and Rosa fill it with miracles!*

He offers us walnuts, from California. Cracking one for himself Fernando says solemnly: *my breakfast is very defined; one walnut, two toasts with olive oil, three toasts with jam, no coffee, chocolate with milk and honey.*

I crack up laughing and pull out my notebook to quote his delightful discipline as Fernando looks up with a twinkle in his eye to ask if I will write this. When I say, *oh yes,* he replies: *then I must break with tradition and crack a second walnut!*

Rosa tells us how unusually cold the weather is this year, and then they both break the news that the bridge between the villages had been swept away years before – but there is a pretty path along the river to the main road which then becomes the Camino. Cross the river there and we are in Palencia. Our encounter is pure serendipity and John decides not to throttle me.

10

A Meseta Moment, Boadilla and Carrión

The walk to Boadilla is long and pretty. This Meseta is the most marvellous of places; it inclines one to reflection. Vanessa and I speak of deep things: her mother-in-law and the bush house with very little in the way of comfort from which she refused to leave in spite of increasing blindness, her dying and her death. I share 2012, my *annus horribilis*. My father had been in a coma for months, his second wife may eventually get to telling me he died. I heard of his stroke through his oldest friend, another exile from father's life with second wife. I went to see him immediately I heard; he was in a hospital hundreds of miles north. I had established a 'suitable' visiting time so as not to collide with second wife. I took him a posy of Cécile Brunner from my rose bush. A Canadian study concluded that the perfume of roses reduces pain, can bring people out of a coma. The nurse, whose name was Lancelot, shook his head and said, *your father is unable to speak*. He was unable to move. I stood by his bed from midday to four o'clock holding the posy by his nose, talking softly, aware of faint flickering of his eyelids, twitching of his nose. Then, in a supreme effort of will, twisting his mouth around words hidden just behind the veil of paralysis, he spoke: *I'm .... so .... glad .... you .... came .... sweetie .... I .... love .... you. Please .... stay .... with .... me.*

I couldn't stay of course, I had nowhere to stay, and the second family would make visiting impossible. Lancelot assured me of *that* when he told me the hospital board was meeting on Monday to override the wife's decision as next of kin to keep my father in *this* hospital for *her* visiting convenience as she didn't drive. It was not a stroke unit and they hadn't the right mattresses or physiotherapy to help alleviate his pain. He told me of my father's condition when he was brought in; unable to walk for months he had been confined to sitting in a chair downstairs in his sitting room and had developed bedsores so deep there was no flesh. I wept. It was the last time I would see my father. Lancelot told me more terrible things too, but as my father's first born of his first marriage I was no longer classed as next-of-kin; I had no rights to protest, to add weight to the argument to move him to more appropriate care. Eventually I learned he was moved to the palliative care of French nuns. This must have been a profound consolation for my father as his adored mother was French. She had died when he was eight. I reflected, once I knew of his transfer, how uncanny his final months, surrounded as his first months of life, by the language of his mother. Neither Vanessa nor I have tears to shed for our memories, tears had fallen and dried long before, and we fall silent. The past walks beside me here ... a clear note in my solitude urges me on.

It was the codicil to this memory of roses that made me give a rose and rosemary to Jüergen for his pain. Those Canadian scientists had crossed the threshold between the discipline of rational science and the intuitive knowledge held by many a mystic that grass is more than green.

Am I examining my own grief as I walk the Meseta? I write screeds in my journal that night in my quiet room in Boadilla, cosied by a hot shower and thick warm bed coverings. I had spent 60 years grieving the absence of my father, my mother had run off with a young swain when I was a child in Singapore, my time for grieving has past. Over the years Jungian analysis and the wisdom of India made sense of my losses, gave me strategies to work with. When my father died I was left not with grief (he suffered so much, death was blessed) but with regret; now he had gone my own hopes, a fantasy no doubt, of ever being included in his life or his largesse had died with him. I recalled a small but telling incident from my whole life of disproportionate family deprivation: many years earlier my father had bought Life Membership to the National Trust for his two boys from family number two – and all the while he was telling me I was puzzling over why not me, too? I was living in a caravan in Stratford upon Avon, so poor a neighbour had given me a sheet to cut up and wear as a maternity dress, and hungry, I was so hungry much of the time, had just suffered the loss of my daughter. My father visited and I had no food to offer him; I had, that day, none for myself. He excused himself to say he would go to the pub for lunch, had brought me a pot plant. He was unable to comprehend my penurious state and I was ignorant of State aid, not having lived in England since I was eleven. I had returned to look for him ...

Little abandoned Boadilla del Camino exists because of Begonia and her beautiful garden, her son, and their joy in welcoming pilgrims. We rest in their oasis, eat homemade almond cake, drink generous cups of tea with lemon. The evening meal is sumptuous, a choice of soups, homemade bread, great tureens of goulash that melt in the mouth, crème caramels and – so I am told – superb wine.

I have a wondrous night's sleep in room 108. John refuses Vanessa's desire to have a room to themselves and insists on the dorm; Vanessa has a shocking night's sleep, snorers again. Too late I remember that I had forgotten to give her extra Ibuprofen.

Walking along the Canal de Fromista in the morning mist is bliss. Yellow iris and water birds lit by the morning light lend an ethereal glow to walkers and the Way. I mostly walk alone, but we catch up in Fromista for *café con leche*, fresh orange juice, a cheese filled croissant and a rest. A modern take on the Last Supper is on the wall of the café, Marilyn Monroe sits central surrounded by the Ratpack, Laurel and Hardy, John Wayne. It makes us smile. So does the answer from the owner when we ask what type of delicious cheese he fills our croissant with. *Generic,* he says. We laugh, and he types into his phone to bring up a translation: *sheep.* Generic sheep's cheese.

We're coming close to the Revenge of the Camino – Revenga de Campos. We choose another detour which in turn leads us to another road rarely travelled, along a river with breezes and chorusing frogs in the reeds, dozens of butterflies and cuckoos. The earth is soft and dry and we are mostly shaded by slender trees along the bank. It is a few miles of pure walking pleasure. Far to our left trails of pilgrims appear antlike on the treeless highway. Many hours pass, we walk separately. The Lovelies need their own space. Mexican standoffs over their last nights' tussle for choice of dorm or room has left Vanessa tired and John decidedly grumpy. I reach a monastery of sorts which has a note on its door welcoming pilgrims to sit and rest in their garden of stone mill wheel tables and tree trunk seats. I remove my boots, cool my feet in *agua sin guarantia sanitaria* from the water pump, put on clean 1000 mile socks, and wait for them to catch up. They take a while. Perhaps I shouldn't have waited. Twos don't need threes even if ones like to be with them. We intend to carry on to Carrión de los Condes, a long long walk totalling 25 kilometres, but stop beforehand to buy lunch. The only bar we find offers bocadillos and the crust is too hard for me to eat. My teeth and feet are a combined story for another day. I walk on without buying a bocadillos, turn a corner and find a whole piazza with tables and chairs under a large awning. I can eat what's on this menu, and do. John and Vanessa find me there, their bocadillos, they tell me, were huge and tasty and satisfying. Vanessa is so tired, and so am I. Detours are lovely but they add to uncalculated mileage and our bodies tell us we have done enough. A short taxi ride will take Vanessa and I to Carrión de los Condes but when we reach the parochial *albergue* a nun comes to meet us to say with real regret – *completo*. She points across the square to a hotel across from the church.

Le Corte is expensive for single guests and, knowing the tensions, I am grateful to share the cost as we take a room for three again. John continued to walk in, catching us up shortly. We wash out socks and tops, hang them on my faithful washing line on the Juliet balcony and go off separately to explore. John has serious blisters and Vanessa is aching so much a pharmacy visit is in order. They return with glowing reports of the caring pharmacist who dresses John's blisters and supplies him with gauze pads and all he needs for a few days; and for Vanessa, Magnesium and Potassium tablets. The pharmacist said: *Ibuprofen? Never!* Shirley MacLaine wrote that she was lacking potassium when she walked, actually ran, she was a driven woman, her Camino. But how would one know one needed such a thing? *Well*, says the pharmacist to Vanessa, *you are walking half marathons every day, your body uses up magnesium and potassium more quickly than it can be replaced during such intense demands on it. The bones are leached of these minerals. You will ache.* Vanessa passes this wisdom on to me, and hands me a couple of tablets too. My bones ache, next stop I must buy the same. I am fascinated by learning this, assess Shirley MacLaine's knowledge as ancillary to her life as an athlete, a dancer, such information must come with the profession. Athletes, more than most people, need to live in their bodies, certainly more than I do. John, much happier now he is out of pain, tells us of a Dutch bereavement agency that recommends walking the Camino as therapy. A kind of living from hour to hour, I think, *extempore*, like birds and angels.

The bathroom in our room has a very short bath, and I have a very long soak. I *do* ache but all I want to do now is eat and sleep.

11

A Taxi, Templars and Terribly Ill

Hmmm, even in a room of three ... John snores. Vanessa, tucked away on the far side, is too tired to notice what is familiar to her anyway. However when she wakes she is still in pain and the pair of us decided to levitate beyond Ledigos – in a taxi. John will walk, he is a 'bush basher' from way back, he says, and has sturdy legs to show for it. We have the kindest driver who sits without his meter ticking while we stop to explore the gorgeous Real Monasterio San Zoilo, an old convent once the court of the Kings of Castille and León, on the way. Sumptuous, cloisters of golden stone, High Gothic, orchards in which to wander, out of the town and in a world of its own; we wished we'd stayed here the night as the *peregrino* price for a three bed suite is so affordable.

The Way all along the road was one we were glad to have missed, no secret ways less travelled here. We pass John striding along the footpath that runs beside the bitumen just about all the way to Terradillos de los Templarios. Another 25 kilometres day for him. Lucky for us we arrive early at this tiny hamlet, population 80, with only two *albergues* and many kilometres further on to the next one. The busy *hospitaleros* are taken aback at our early arrival, tell us to leave our packs in lockers in an adjacent room and to return to register at midday. The gardens are lovely, the grass inviting, and we lay down to rest.

In due time we book our bunks in the grand sounding *Jacques du Molay*, he who was the 23rd Grand Master of the Knights

Templar. He had died a shocking death and I wondered at his connection with this tiny place. Recalling that there is a famous Templar castle along the Camino somewhere Vanessa and I go to find it. In less time than it takes to say *Jacques du Molay* we have left the village. No castle appears. We try another path from the *albergue* to find a black donkey with eyes that hold the sadness of all donkeys ever abused by man, but no castle. I admit defeat and we stroll about for an hour or so before returning to the Templar name with no castle; not even a Templar grave on which is inevitably carved a knight with his legs crossed to show he'd sliced a Saracen or two. There we lay on our backs with our legs up against a tree trunk in the tranquil garden again; patches of sun between clouds keep the temperature mild, the air so dry it would cure parchment. I lay here wondering if I'll bother putting my journal notes into a book, who would be interested in reading yet another Camino chronicle? My thoughts drift with the clouds above me and a would-be title pops into my head: *Same Skirt, Different Day* by Poppy Peregrina. I love it and turn my head to tell Vanessa. She is sound asleep.

Late in the afternoon John arrives and countless other tired pilgrims are turned away, some look exhausted. John says it was not a pleasant walk, and he can walk anywhere. Vanessa and I are glad we followed our instincts. I have a not very nice chicken soup for lunch, little except water from the pots of boiling chicken being prepared for the evening meal, with the addition of a barley seed floating in it. I decide not to eat in the evening but Vanessa has the chicken stew and John has the other dish offered. Once John arrives we are definitely a two and a one again and I go to sit at a table to write while they choose the grass and gather around them other pilgrims.

Everyone has one Bad Day on the Camino. I wake to beautiful weather, begin to walk through beautiful country, redolent with the intense scent of broom from hedgerows eight feet high planted as a baffle between the Camino path and the busy main road. I walk more and more slowly, pain and nausea bring me almost to a standstill but I put one foot in front of the other, lean on my walking stick, lurch into an uneven balance while my head disengages from my body which is down there somewhere crying out for attention.

Every step is agony. The Lovelies are far ahead, the morning rush of pilgrims has long passed me by, my hips almost crumble.

After many miles walking in a kind of delirium I stop. At that instant Vanessa, a distant speck, must have sensed something seriously amiss. She turns back. A goodly wait and she reaches me. She stays with me, step by slow step, and we make it to the mediaeval bridge and the twelfth century Hermitage of Our Lady of the Bridge. John is waiting on the other side. Once over it I fall down heavily on the grass in front of the ruined Hermitage. I can no longer move. Sahagun is another 3 kilometres or so. After a while Vanessa props me up, John takes my pack, and somehow I reach the first hotel at this edge of the town; a hotel with a grand foyer and a sympathetic receptionist who takes in the scene in front of him at once. He calls a taxi. Vanessa comes with me and just as well for by the time we reach Bercianos del Real Camino we both fall out of the taxi. She is also very ill.

I fall in a heap on the front steps of the *albergue* and Vanessa lays flat out on the bench by the old stone wall of this impressive building. The door opens. An American says the *albergue* is closed until 2 o'clock. I hear it but can't move. Vanessa is out of it. Then I hear a very English voice exclaim in dismay and I look up. Obviously we *are* ill. Spinning through my brain is the blessed coincidence of meeting two English speaking *hospitaleros*. Though speaking is not necessary now as David produces mattresses for us to lay in the garden until opening time and Patricia tells me she is from Shalford. Synchronicity indeed. Who would have heard of tiny Shalford unless they know it personally? Old and dear friends of mine from Father Bede and Shantivanam days live in Shalford, which is a bend more or less between Godalming and Guildford. Later I learn that Greece and Australia link Patricia and I too – but first this handsome couple are off to Sahagun to shop for the evening pilgrim meal and will leave us to sleep in the garden.

The garden begins to fill with pilgrims, John arrives, and 2 o'clock comes. I am carried in by John and Patricia upstairs to a small room of two by two bunks. Vanessa manages to walk upstairs. We each collapse. Patricia brings in bowls for us to vomit in, tells us we must stay two nights to recover. Suddenly Vanessa throws up, spectacularly; three days worth of food three times in succession. Later I manage to throw up the gruel I had eaten at Terradillos. John is so kind. Patricia tells us a number of pilgrims arrive ill from Terradillos; those who had eaten chicken at Jacques du Molay. Vanessa says their kitchen was spotless and we conclude it was more likely to have been the source of the chicken, a diseased fowl perhaps, which has caused what is, most likely, food poisoning.

Patricia is a joy and delight, pops up to check on us and talk. She and David met on the Camino last year, knew it was a meant-to-be meeting, stayed together, learned Spanish for four months in Peru or somewhere, applied to be *hospitaleros* at this beautiful parochial *albergue* and had arrived two days beforehand for their two week volunteering. How's that for timing – we laugh well over our own good fortune at meeting. Patricia wants to live in Australia, hopes David will warm to the idea too when they go later in the year. Meeting Australian Lovelies adds to the amalgam of synchronicities that touch each of us. Through my haze of unwellness I register that Vanessa and Patricia are quite beautiful, and their beloveds well matched. John helps to make up the bunks as a kindness to Patricia and David for giving us an extra day and night to recover our strength.

75

I have been walking for 22 days, 354 kilometres less a couple of short lifts. Two days rest and we are well enough to move on. Vanessa and John will walk and I may not see them again. In my heart I am sad at saying goodbye, they are special, my Camino enriched by knowing them. I wish, fleetingly, I still had a life in Australia, they would surely be part of it. I, with the wisdom of Caroline's Camino before me, and still feeling too wobbly to walk the distances demanded today, decide to take a taxi to León, offering to carry the hefty *mochila's* of two charming young men who intend walking the entire 45 kilometres in one go, *today*. I name the younger Frenchman Johnny Depp and he poses to perfection with pirate hat, cockle shell and large mafia sunglasses. They have walked from Le Puy, travelling long distances every day.

John had sat at their table last night and commented later that the young Frenchman's good manners at dinner showed up a graceless Australian with whom John was ashamed of being associated as being a fellow Oz. Emiliano, the older of the two, is enormously grateful for my offer of transport for the *mochilas*. He is sitting on the bench, looks woeful. Blisters are troubling him. Johnny Depp is upbeat, would charm the gold from his grandmother's teeth.

My taxi driver is a delight, expresses concern that I walk alone, is astonished that I have walked from Pamplona, drops me at the door of the hotel Patricia recommends for being exactly behind the Cathedral. He smiles warmly, shakes my hand, wishes me *buen camino* and leaves me to my fate.

12

León, León, León

Standing outside the hotel Q!H I look up at the golden stone of the great Cathedral, sense the atmosphere of the people passing and instantly fall in love with León. But first, a little drama. The hotel is full. Every hotel is full, there is a mediaeval fare in León this weekend and today is Friday. Half of Spain is here in this city to enjoy or participate in the re-enactment of the coming of the Roman Legions to León in 29 BC. I look with dismay at Johnny Depp's 18 kilograms *mochila,* and at Emiliano's 12 kilograms *mochila,* and at my probably 6 kilograms *mochila,* and wonder how on earth ... The receptionist rescues me, *leave them all here* she says, *go and find a hotel.*

I quash my panic; a part of me manages a wry smile as a favourite aphorism pops into my head and dances time with my footsteps: *no good deed goes unpunished.* How on earth was I going to shift such weights and where on earth was a hotel that had a room?

After a Very Long Time, and endless wandering, I leave the mediaeval part of the city altogether and cross a large piazza to chance upon a hotel and enter the astonishing art deco lobby and phenomenal stairwell of Alfonso V. Oh my! They have one double room left, and let me have it at the *peregrina* price of 50€ a night. It is a four star hotel. I take it, return to Q!H, they ring me a taxi to transport everything and, uh oh, I meet the most foul-tempered taxi driver in Spain! He does not want to lift what I certainly can't into the boot of his cab. I gesture, *forget it, I'll get another taxi*, and his snarl clearly indicates his greed for a fare. *No good deed goes unpunished*, I could easily have carried my own *mochila* and walked, but the transport of the other two cost me a rip off, and this unpleasant man refuses to carry them into the lobby of Alfonso V! Abandoning them on the road he drives off quick smart and leaves me to run up the grand staircase to ask the hotel doorman to help. *What*, was written across the doorman's forehead, *is this woman doing with multiples of such vast mochilas?* And that proves a sticking point. Mine was welcome of course, and being carried by a Virgo it was pristine, but *these,* the receptionist behind the counter curls his lip in distaste, looks at the two *mochilas* as two remnants having rolled in from Roland's eighth century battlefield of Roncesvalles, *these* were not fit to remain in *his* lobby...

Imploring both reluctant hotel staff to hold them on the ground floor for the lads I then run back to Q!H to leave cross-references for the whereabouts of their *mochila's* as Q!H – our point of contact – wouldn't keep them in *their* lobby. Oh, no good deed goes unpunished, this unpromising start to my rapturous love affair with León has taken up four *hours* of my first day. And I needed food, seriously.

The brasserie attached to the Q!H solves that dilemma. Now I can enjoy my explorations. Rounding the corner into the Cathedral Square I bump into two glamorous gals from Scottsdale wearing Macabis. Another American *peregrina* with her husband takes photos. Our skirts, the ugliest garment ever created, are simply the best invention for walkers, *ever.*

León is utterly gorgeous. And the Cathedral, oh my! No wonder it is named *Pulchra Leonina*, the House of Light. Alas my camera fails me here. The Cathedral is reminiscent of Sainte-Chapelle in Paris and quite simply the most beautiful Gothic stone poem in the world. It is Light, bringing Light. Vast stained glass windows, mostly with their original mediaeval glass, divided by stone tracery, sit above those below, an internal division of upper and lower chapels of windows upon windows. The entire interior is rippled by colour pouring through the two-tiered windows. The vaulted ceiling so high and so sublime I confess I stepped inside – and cried. It is too beautiful to find words for. It holds me in a kind of rapture. I return to the guide to ask for the audio earphones and listen to its long history, its life and hard times, its miracle of survival as the foundations began to crumble some few hundred years ago, it having been built over Roman foundations. I recognise a Greek name honoured as its saviour stonemason in the fifteenth century, called in by the Benedictines who were the Cathedral custodians. To miss this wonder would be cause for regret – just being here is a sublime experience. Like all ancient places of prayer and quietude the stones hold memory; *déjà vu* comes not from the tiny human mind remembering, but the depth charge of stones re-membering *us*. In this case – *me*. I felt it in Şanliurfa (ancient Edessa), in Harran, in Epidaurus, in Men-an-Tol. I could write of many others but *now* I am enchanted with León.

As I wander round the ambulatory I come to another astonishment – a pregnant Mary; Virgin Mary *parturient*. I *am* astonished. The statue is pretty well life-size, her face has been carved with an expression of such wistfulness as would make any mother weep, as if in expectant knowing of how she would lose her child in a particularly brutal way. This has nothing to do with religion, but echoes the human anguish we can all feel when someone we know loses a beloved child.

Later, replete, I wander through the setting up of the weekend's huge fair, marvel at what stalls I can see already, buy samples of cakes, am told to pose for a photograph by the artisan breads of a young woman baker from Galicia, and return to my wondrous room to wash me and my clothes in the marble bathroom, string up my line on the balcony, and hang out my *peregrina* outfit to dry. By now I am feeling rather off-colour again, though the gold embroidered monogram of Alfonso V on the pillowcases and the shower curtain – how decadent is that, a gold *embroidered* monogram on a shower curtain – bring a smile to my tired face. This is an unfamiliar luxury in my life and I silently thank my Secret Agent once more.

Fast forward to finish this day's story – the lads arrived exhausted around 6pm. They had been walking for 12 hours. Because he wasn't burdened with his own *mochila* Johnny Depp had carried the *mochila* of an elderly, limping pilgrim they met in Reliegos for the last 25 kilometres. Emiliano's blisters are raw now, and he looks so woebegone sitting there in the grand lobby as the receptionist goes to retrieve their *mochilas*. *Aren't you using NOK*, I say, surprised. *What's NOK*, he asks. Johnny Depp whips his from his pocket. Taken aback I ask the Arrogance of Youth why he hasn't told his friend, who is Italian and doesn't know about NOK, about this French miracle. With a Gallic shrug (the one that says everyone else is a fool) he answers: *he wants to use Vaseline*. As if that is reason enough not to enlighten his friend. I shake my head; at least the good deed had resulted in another pilgrim having his *mochila* lifted from his back for his walk. I tell Emiliano to filch Johnny Depp's NOK before he walks another step, though shutting the stable door after the horse has bolted won't solve his flayed feet now.

It has been a full day. I sleep more than well under the thick duvet on my excellent bed, covered by cotton sheets of at least 500 thread count. Bliss.

13

A Day of Wonders

I wake immensely refreshed with both a thought and a feeling clamouring for attention. The feeling was easy to locate, my skin. During all the days on the Meseta, which runs between Burgos and León, the air was so dry it would cure parchment; it does bear repeating because my poor nose suffered too. I was desiccated inside and out. All juices dried, my nose felt like a crisp, if I attempted to blow out the crisp my nose would bleed. Such a nuisance! Give me woman weather I thought, moist, soft as silk on the skin, *humid,* winter in tropical Townsville is just about perfection, England has its share of humidity too, in all seasons. This morning my skin feels perfect again, and I can breathe well. I look through the window – there has been rain in the night.

The thought, an intuition really, was insistent: I must phone the Lovelies. John had given me his mobile number just in case. I found it and at 7 o'clock went down to reception to ask if I could call. Vanessa answered, her voice a sob of gratitude. *I have just ended my prayers to the Green Tara for help and you ring! You are the answer to my prayer. We are in Reliegos, it's horrid, John spent the night vomiting, we've been refused a second day, the hospitalero told us to leave, the walk from Bercianos was dreadful and every hotel I phoned in León is full. I have exhausted all possibilities.*

I ask her to wait two seconds, cover the phone and ask the receptionist if he has a double room. *No, we are fully booked,* he says, *but there is one suite, just one, for 100€ a night.* I relay this to Vanessa. *Get a taxi* I say, *just get here, the receptionist will give you 5 minutes to confirm your booking.* She has to ask John. Duh. Sure enough as soon as I replace the phone it rings, someone wants the suite. The good receptionist says he will return their call in five minutes, replaces the receiver and the phone rings again. It is Vanessa. They are on their way. The receptionist returns the call of the unlucky caller. León is full to capacity.

Well pleased with the morning I head off to Q!H for their excellent breakfast. Alfonso's breakfast, reputedly lavish, is really too costly for one person; it is priced as a special offer for the same cost for two. By 8.30 I am at the Cathedral cloisters waiting to go in to the museum. Weather is wet, windy and chilly. A priest pushes open the huge door and goes through. I blithely follow. He walks along the cloisters and turns left. So do I. We come to a side chapel where another priest is offering Mass. After Mass all leave but I hover unnoticed for half an hour in the quiet of the cloisters. I am cold, I brought so few clothes as June is supposed to be warm, but I rub my arms hopefully and take the time to examine the carvings and the decorative cloister ceiling. When the door officially opens I appear from the inside to pay the entrance fee. Led back the way I had been the ticket seller unlocks an ancient door, invites me inside, locks the door behind me and turns on the lights of each of the four floors. She smiles, and locks me in as she leaves.

Four floors of beauty and art; one thousand years of priceless treasures of inestimable value all created for the Divine and rescued from time, terrorism, neglect, plunder – all so lovingly housed here. My adored Virgins in Majesty, some so worm ridden, so small, so damaged, so hieratic, so calm – their smiles, winks, directness, gaze, sorrow make a seamless silent coloratura of emotion everywoman knows. There is no photography permitted, and my camera fails me anyway, unable to focus in such poor light. I don't use flash but I do attempt a couple of photos as I am so moved by certain faces.

The anguish of St John as he supports Holy Mary over the pieta of her dead son is so shockingly human, so intense, my own mouth moves in pity; I stand in my own grief for her. The Angel leading Tobias with his fish, his little dog running alongside is a panel of innocence and poignancy on a staircase wall, and almost missed. The ethereal lightness of the faces of mediaeval Angels in carved wood and polychrome; St Lucy, St Catherine, St Anne teaching Mary as a child – all touch me, and all are displayed sensitively.

However, the disembowelling of St Erasmus under the leering faces of the watchers and of the holders of the turnspit I found almost too horrific to register until I realize I am also looking at Blessed Richard Whiting, the last Abbot of Glastonbury, also hung, drawn, quartered and disembowelled alive at the age of 80 during the 'Reformation' *twelve hundred years* later. The Age of Cruelty, parallel to the Age of Beauty, seems a long long time in human centuries.

A priest comes in from an internal door to let me out just as I reach the last stair down. Outside in the grand square I am back in ordinary time.

It is now late morning and I return to Alfonso. Today I intend buying a lighter *mochila*. I enter the foyer just as the Lovelies are signing in. Vanessa fairly flies to me and envelopes me in her arms to thank me. John's green and Queen Victoria face – not amused – tells me all I need not to know. He heads upstairs, disinterested with the demi-miracle of his wife's prayer and my phone call to extricate him from a situation Vanessa was too exhausted to negotiate. Gratitude, for John, was not the word of the moment. I chuckle to myself, take the lift to my floor, get out from the fridge the cakes I'd bought yesterday and ran back down to give them to Vanessa as a welcome.

83

Then I'm off again. First to buy a super light *mochila* from Roberto down in La Rua street. He offers me a shocking pink Deuter complete with yellow lily, just for gals, or electric blue. I cringe and tell him I cannot wear colours louder than the landscape. He thoroughly approves and goes backstage to find me a cream and fawn Ferrino Durance 32 Womens of which I thoroughly approve. He takes a long time to fit it well, tells me it is a well-respected Italian make of some provenance amongst mountaineers. I giggle, *bathos*, I think as I imagine me unable to even climb the Tor with a packed lunch. It is a lovely encounter and I am happy with the result. I take my new *mochila* back to my room and scoot back out again. I'm off to the Fair via a brief visit to St Francis in the Park, a nodding acknowledgement of serpents to signify apothecaries, a smile for the bubble blower in the street, a life size street bronze of an old man on a park bench. An amalgam of charms that make up this marvellous city of León as I make my way to the Fair.

I arrive just as the Roman Legions march in to disturb the local shepherds and goatherds with their shaggy goatskin bagpipes. This Fair is a huge affair, running along all the mediaeval side streets, filling all the squares with gaiety and colour and irresistible smells. I make my way to the Pulpo and Piglet marquee to watch entranced for more than half an hour as a master chef creates a splendid *paella*. Each single ingredient is placed by hand, positioned on the bubbling rice and broth base in perfect patterns; giant prawns, langoustines, clams, mussels, tiny shellfish of different kinds, all added according to the timing necessary for cooking, one by one. I am impressed. He is impressed with my attention. Finally it is covered and steamed and I wait. Chef serves me a wondrous portion for my patience, with every tasty morsel I had been watching transform over the flames of his alchemy. *For you, Senora,* he smiles, *buen appetito*. I sit at a table and eat blissfully and messily and one of the family comes to wipe my hands with a substantial length of blue paper towel.

Too late I find a street market that had been given over to antiques and *brocante* and was packing up, but not quickly enough to hide a treasure. Oh! Oh! I fall in love with a small roundel of the Virgin and Child in a pastoral scene; exquisite and too well painted to be called kitsch. *I want! I want!* my heart cries, and the vendor pounced! Alas, I don't have the amount of cash and he doesn't take cards. I also have a backpack and a further 350 kilometres to walk – *get real gal!* The imponderables are insurmountable. I take a photo, with his permission, instead. I shall regret not bringing her home with me as much as I regret not trying to struggle home with the majolica Madonna water stoop that claimed my heart in Positano some years ago. Ah well.

I walk down Avenida San Marcos to the old pilgrim hospital, now the most splendid of all paradors in Spain. A suite for a week costs my annual income. I wander everywhere, invisible. I have a knack for withdrawing energy, taught to me by an Inuit shaman from north of Nome whom I met while in Santa Fe way back in 1988. He sat invisible on the fender of his car, watching me look everywhere for him – he was teaching me traditional ways of communication with the natural world around us, using the elements of which we are also made up – until he suddenly 'reappeared'. I've never managed his degree of invisibility of course, but I can move unseen when I choose to. I chose to right now and wandered entranced far beyond the access granted to non-guests. The twelfth century building is immensely beautiful, its art and statuary magnificent. I rue the loss of it for pilgrims such as I, but appreciate its protection as an invaluable piece of Spanish history and heritage. A wedding, the perfect couple, a perfect setting, his surname, I read on the Paradorés invitation, is Ángel. May their marriage be blessed by them. I slip out as silently as I had entered.

Along San Marcos Street I have a sublime green apple and chestnut homemade ice cream. Now I return to their café to *indulge,* without a nano-second of guilt shadowing my tea and *petit four,* and bring out my journal to write of the day and my thoughts. I take photos of this extravagantly beautiful shop whose cakes and window display and wall paintings nourish the heart and soul as well as the body and senses and get to wondering. Ah, the *senses.* That's the conundrum ... *sensual.* Too self-indulgent, too sensual, too glorious – so *Catholic!* I found shops like this all over France and Italy, and now Spain. Do we English create such pure indulgent fantasy and feasts for the *senses?* Grandeur, yes. Gardens, yes. But Pure Indulgence? What is the common denominator for France and Italy and Spain? I challenge my brain. Ping! It's obvious – no Puritanism, no guilt, no self-abnegation, no unhealthy boarding school sniggering at sexuality, devoid of *sensuality* – ha, the list is endless. Cromwell's Puritans *banned mince pies,* can you credit it, and Christmas, and pilgrimages. Imagine anything so punitive! Charles ll, with a brief brave nod at the temporary return of Catholicism (though mindful of the regicide of his father for his true faith) re-instated them. I enjoy my little raves, love my journal, it lives with my *credencial* in my Macabi pocket, more valuable than my passport and privy to the deeper verities that inform my place in the world.

Still the day is not yet over. There is a cello concert by an American pilgrim at San Isidore in the evening. I miss it; I am waiting at the wrong door. Photographing a statue of a very raggedy and rusty *peregrina* in a hat and skirt, who looks like I might look by the time I reach Santiago, I catch sight of a poster for a *Son et Lumière* to be performed right here this evening at 9 o'clock. The grand façade of San Isidore will be its 'canvas'. By chance I meet Vanessa who insists I follow her back to see a wondrous stone Madonna in her deep vaulted *camarin* of stars. I tell her of the *Son et Lumière. What's that?* she asks and I don't explain, just urge her to fetch John from his death bed, it is not to be missed. It proves a stunning show. French illuminator Xavier de Richemont has created breath-stopping beauty of the history of León and we are entranced, thrilled, moment by illuminated moment.

Vanessa thanks me for the beginning and the end of a perfect day for her. We walk home together to Alfonso. It has been a Day of Wonders.

14

An Angel at the Crossroads

I wake well on Sunday, pack and prepare everything and then go downstairs to invent *poppyperegrina at gmail.com* on the hotel computer. I am highly resistant to google-world-domination and in case you feel the same resistance to its limitations (if someone or something isn't google-bound, so I discovered, it will not appear in your searches) I pass on my favourite dog, Arfie. I'm a cat woman myself, but Arfie, who is the sleuth hound of *www.dogpile.com* is the mastermind behind all search engines and fetches things from places ungenerous google won't. I've been using Arfie for twenty years, he never lets me down. But, needs must, and though I can't recall more than two email addresses I feel better for having a toehold back in cyber space, just in case.

Alfonso V was the perfect two night pause. I am rejuvenated and ready to walk. In her own good time the newly created Poppy Peregrina pops on her much lighter *mochila*, gathers up staff and hat and sallies forth down San Marcos. Oh my! The divine café of the green apple and chestnut ice cream is open even though it is Sunday. I go in for breakfast – *té con limon* and a mini hot-from-the-oven flan the likes of which lightness I have not tasted before. These people know how to make pastry. I ask for another one to take for my journey but, in spite of how early, they've all gone. Just as I was hearing this their baker walks in with another fresh tray full. I buy, resist reluctantly the green apple ice cream, and quietly slip out: *buen Camino*, they call as I leave with my picnic.

I walk on down to the splendid parador San Marcos and go in to have my *credencial* stamped. The *sello* isn't as grand as some, but as I stand there I am set upon by the wealthy with splendid cameras. Please can they photograph a real *peregrina*, they ask. I obligingly smile for various Dutch and Australian tourists who wish me well and tell me how brave I am and an inspiration. I agree with everything and an Australian woman of a similar age walks me to the bridge to wave me goodbye. I take my leave of lovely León and far on my way I pass a huddle of hobbit houses whose only evidence is a door in the side of the hill. I think they might be bodegas.

I walk on and on, to arrive at La Virgen del Camino where I ask the way as I seem to have lost a cockleshell or two during my directions. I am pointed far down the street to a fast highway and road bridge. I eventually reach it to find another possibility. An Angel is at the crossroads reading a huge cardboard painted sign propped up against a tree. The sign is as big as me. Two divergent roads are marked in red and black. Injunctions like: *Go For Nature* and *Embark on the Adventure* and *Camino Alternativo Por La Naturaleza* really give me no choice but to take the road less travelled once more. Peering at the board the Angel turns and says, *well this must be it*. We look at each other and turn left, heading for the Adventure.

I travel with Angel the whole day. She is a delight, a very conscious and aware hip-hop gal from San Francisco who has been walking for nearly two months. Her parents, a little younger than me, are ahead. They wake earlier than Angel and as she is at the point of divorcing them they wisely decided the better part of valour is to keep 20 kilometres between each other. She makes me smile with her wonderful observations and good humour. She is thirty-one, works in an Outdoor Store. Her parents have walked the Camino before; decide to do it again so they can take Angel too. The three began their Camino in Porto, Portugal, reach Santiago, achieve their

Compostelas, then stride on to Finisterre, Muxia and back to Santiago –and receive more *Compostelas*. Angel thought she was going home then. She had been walking over a month. But no, her parents broke the news that all three were taking a train to Pamplona to walk back along the Camino Frances to – Santiago. Angel felt justified in proposing a divorce.

The road to Fresno is pure Meseta; long, flat and red earthed. Herbs perfume the way: thyme, marjoram, oregano. Their oil is pungent as we brush past. Clouds shelter the sun from burning us, and Angel gives me a dollop of sunscreen. I am so glad to share her company. We stop at Chozas de Abajo, a blink of a watering hole that sells excellent coffee at its one bar. Many miles later we arrive at Villar de Mazarife, I am charmed by the welcoming appearance of the municipal *albergue* but equally gladly follow Angel to Tio Pepe where her parents have booked a room. As it happens Tio Pepe is *completo* but for the top bunk in the room with Angel's parents. All is well. They are delightful, they'd have to be wouldn't they, to name their daughter Angel.

The top bunk proves difficult. The stool to step on is a metre short of purchase! I need a ladder; I am tired; the ladder is not forth-coming and I am standing on very tired legs at the foot of the bunks while the other three rest. Angel, being a good nine inches taller than me, is able to heave herself up. I prevail upon the *albergue* owner for steps. *Yes*, she says, and does nothing. After a deal of time I go back down to her, brace myself at the bar and say: *Senora! I have walked over 400 kilometres from Pamplona, I am almost old, and I am very tired. I need to lie down on my bed and I need a ladder NOW!* Suddenly she finds a key, a shed, a step ladder. Just like that.

We four ate our pilgrim meal together, it was mediocre. I take family photos for them with their camera by the statue, and Angel takes one of me with my camera. In the corner store I buy a large tube of rich rose hip moisturizer for a ridiculously low price (€1.49) to discover it is made from organic rose hips collected from the hedgerows. It lasts me all the way home, and I use it liberally over all of me every day. The storks high on the bell tower just beyond our window clack and settle down for the night.

Nancy and Vern leave silently at 6 am, they will walk all the way to Astorga, I calculate that in kilometres, it must surely be thirty-five at least. Angel and I have a coffee, hug warmly as we go forth and the day unfolds. I walk on happily. It seems a long way to Villavente where pilgrims are sitting outside a small café. I recognise Sandy and Gene from Tampa, it was Sandy who photographed the Three Macabi's in León. Mary and Eamon from Ireland are young and beautiful, *very* beautiful. American Dan and Esther share stories – Dan grew so many veggies he went to offer the excess to the local women's refuge for victims of domestic violence. It was a very secretive transaction, for months he was met in the street and refused closer contact. He is a man after all. Eventually he became so trusted he was allowed to deliver the veggies to their door *and* ask the cook what she would like for the next day. Esther is a GP and speaks Spanish.

We reach Hospital de Órbigo with its spectacular mediaeval bridge, the longest mediaeval bridge in the world and still cobbled. Only a thousand people live in the village – I'd be happy to add me as an additional statistic, it is charming. Half way across the bridge is a sign board with text and painting. Esther began translating the positively endless shaggy dog story of the legend behind the Puente de Passo Honroso. Dan and I can't bear it any longer and keep saying: *but did he get his girl?* And at the point where Esther says: *No, he didn't,* we both groan – and walk on. Minutes later Esther, who read though to the last full stop, joins us smiling: *yes he did get his girl,* she said, *years later after walking the Camino as a peregrino!*

From here I had planned to go on to Villares de Órbigo to a new and recommended *albergue* but can't pass the wondrous parochial *albergue* here in Hospital with its blue shutters and courtyard of delights, tiled *fuente* and Maltese Cross in the cobbles. The Knights of Malta founded the hospital here, legacy of their role as Knights Hospitallers; they who founded the first hospital on Rhodes and along whose battlements I would walk during the years of my Greek Tragedy. I ask for a single room, oh joy! they have such a wonder, and, up crooked stairs and past warrens of rooms marked *privado,* I am led to an alcove of two rooms each with a double bed. I am thrilled, €15 and sleeping alone.

Now I am in the best restaurant, still accompanied by Angels, *Los Ángeles.* I order trout soup, the waiter approves of my choice, *típica Hospital de Órbiga,* he smiles, and delicately peels and bones the trout for me. I lower my head and smile broadly to myself as I recall a Kurd gallant in Urfa shaking his head in quiet amusement over my smoked *patlican* kebab – he came to my rescue too, delicately peeling away the smoke toughened skin of the aubergine. Duh - can't trust a foreigner, *el Inglése,* to know these refinements! The crème caramel drew the waiter's approval too, *casa speciality.*

I return to the Knights of Malta to find a tired young lad from Fowey – he is *skateboarding* to Santiago. *How did you manage to climb Alto del Perdón? Negotiate down those rocky paths to Uterga? I* ask, aghast. *Difficult,* he said. *Difficult! But not Impossible? I* gasp, astonished. Gabriella, the multi-linguistic Hungarian *hospitalera* of the moment laughs hugely and translates to all and sundry, causing much merriment. I reflect on Francois and his donkey; the charioteer family; the littlest pilgrim, right here in his carrier; Yves with his wheelie pulley; Simone and her socks and sandals; the beautiful flaxen plaited NZ woman walking with her *eight* children; the young Italian girl and her dog – and other pilgrims with burdens of the heart, Christine, Karel, Peter-Paul... the Camino brings us all together. The woman in the shop where I bought fruit tells me her son is in Canterbury, teaching *basketball*. Really this Camino gets curiouser and curiouser. I *love* this adventure!

I pick an Annunciation lily struggling to find light in the tangle of roses in the churchyard and put her by my bed in the toothbrush glass. I even have my own sink – though I now discover sink an apt word for the mattress which has collapsed under the weight of a thousand Knights – in full armour. Resourceful as ever I see that out in the corridor between my blue shutters and the outer wall with windows to fresh air stands a MDF bed sized board amongst a load of discarded stuff. With stealth and innovative thinking I devise a strategy to manoeuvre this hefty piece through the blue shutters into my room. I balance it by inches as I run between the corridor and bedroom via the bathroom and back again a few times to edge it through. Miraculously it fits through the window, lands on one edge with a thump and I position another edge against the side window jamb. Then I run back round to the bedroom to upend the sunken mattress – very tricky, it almost folds up on itself it is so devoid of support and won't remain on its side. More juggling, and the board plops on to the sunken springs, I drop the mattress, and voila! a bed!

Well satisfied I go into the wild garden, greet two cats and sit by the old bush of fragrant *noisette* roses by the stream. Roses and poppies will ever remain for me symbolic of the Camino. The house, however, is little short of a hovel but is so charming, so full of character, that each unstable floorboard is in truth singing a song of pilgrim feet.

Pipiéna is the magnificent coloured Frenchwoman in the room next to mine and is walking the Camino in stages. I can hardly believe I am over half way, have walked nearly 500 kilometres. I must have bi-located.

Left early. Pipiéna gives me a huge hug and kiss and *bon chemin*. I take the road less travelled again, aided by a group of super fit Germans who call me back from heading off on neither of the right roads at all. The path runs along a canal and a heady tang of ox-eye and michaelmas daisies, cut hay and wild lavender add to the sensual sound of water, the sight of red earth, fields and asphodel, far hills and oh! snow caps! A few more steps and beyond the spurs of golden furze unfolds a whole panorama of mountains. I am headed for those – the thought is exhilarating, not because I particularly love mountains or snow but because I have walked through every terrain along 500 kilometres! I have *walked*! The thought is breathtaking and tears of astonishment prickle my eyes.

I stop at a café in Santibáñez de Valdeiglesias, the signpost is larger than the hamlet. The café is sparkling and I am pleased my intuition led me away from the dreary TV pounding bar in Villares. The coffee is strong and rich. Two weary women sit at the table next to me. I am perky from a good night's sleep and I ask where they have walked from. I suspect I have a little smugness lurking behind the question, but pride comes before a complete collapse as my jaw hits the deck at their answer! *Luxembourg,* they say, *we are a little tired today, we have walked 2340 kilometres, we begin on March 20th with two rest days only. Three months and albergues all the way, though in France they are different.* It is now the 10th of June.

I am humbled by these women, who may be their late thirties, but could be any age really, they look so well, tired, but quietly glowing. I look a hundred and seventy these days. Mariette carries a pack and Marianne wheels a *randonée* chariot like Yves. As if to downplay their own astonishing achievement they open the newspaper on the counter to show me the photo of a French pilgrim in a *wheelchair* passing through León. He pushes only with his hands. I am brought to dust, my own wheelchair-and-almost-seventy story stops right here.

I never mention either again. My Camino is a walk in the park by comparison.

I walk on and on, up hills and down dales, alone with all the nature I love. Up the last hill and there in front of me is a long low red mud brick structure of three sides and little else. By the path is a blue cart covered by a cheery canvas tarp and a young man who calls: *Welcome to Paradise!*

15

Cornucopia, Chocolates and Cello

Welcome to Paradise calls the young man, inviting me to sample his cornucopia of delights: homemade ginger biscuits, organic homemade bread, every organic fruit jam including guava – *guava* for goodness sake, on a blue cart in the middle of the Meseta – peanut and almond butters, dried fruits, fresh fruits in great bowls, a melon being cut just as my mouth forms a silent O of astonishment.

Andreas tells me he is from Romania, walked the Camino some years back, wanted to return to give back to the Camino some of the magic he had received. We agree Bucegi and the Carpathian mountains are magnificent and no, I didn't see a bear, though there were signs everywhere. I am talking in order to inject something known into such an unknowable scenario so I can grasp my threadbare sense of reality. I also eat; that's real. Then I offload my pack and sit down. It's all too marvellous. The more I walk this astonishing trail called Camino the more I feel like Alice in Wonderland. I have an interesting exchange with Kathy, a South African who wears a terrific red sunhat, take a couple of photos as more pilgrims arrive. Andreas encourages everyone by saying Astorga is only 6 kilometres further on and downhill all the way. The five tier pedestrian pass zig-zagging over the road is impressive and practical.

The Wonderland of Alice becomes more surreal as I am welcomed into the huge *albergue* by the *hospitalero*; an elderly *Japanese* from Abergavenny – in *Wales*! I'm shown into a room

96

of four; already in there are Mary and Eamon, last met in Villavente. I vaguely wondered why Eamon's hair is seven shades lighter, but Mary's thick chestnut plait is a bulwark against doubt – until she introduces herself as Louise and her husband as Hugh. My confusion is as thick as the coffee I treat myself to later in the town.

I had a one handed cold shower – that's all there is – which helps the neurons resettle their confusion: small brain, infinite wisdom, slow to compute. Then I'm off to the rose garden adjacent to the *albergue* to sit on a wall and eat my picnic before exploring Astorga.

Alas the chocolate factory was closed, the Cathedral was closed, Gaudi's Bishop's Palace was closed. No wonder the bronze statue aptly named Quo Vadis outside the *albergue* door is carrying off his suitcase in high feather!

Astorga defies all my attempts at affection. To restore my *sangfroid* I lay on the warm grass in front of the Bishop's Palace for an hour or so. Wandering across the square later I met Dane Johansen. What can I say? This most personable young man is an inspiration. He is walking from St Jean Pied de Port to Finisterre carrying his 11 kilograms cello on his back. Sometimes he walks 40 kilometres in a day! He lobs into an *albergue* like the rest of us, has cold showers if that's all that's on offer, rests a while and then gives an hour's performance in every church and Cathedral along the Way. That's a prodigious feat! Tonight he will give a concert of cello music by the Cathedral. My Alice in Wonderland moments only need a white rabbit...

The concert was marvellous, many familiar faces were there, Dane shared that his 30th birthday was the previous night. What a gifted young man, and how the Spanish all along the route have encouraged advertising his pilgrimage and concerts. Many many of the audience were local people too.

I've seen the posters, but until now have missed him by a day, or, in León, by a church door, wherever I've been.

Tomorrow – will I make it to Rabanal I wonder, it is another long walk of 20 kilometres, with a high-ish climb rising to 1150 metres. When morning comes we are woken by Gregorian chant and I find I am walking out with Dane and Angel and her parents as far as the pretty village of Murias de Rechivaldo. I do not stay for coffee but note the lovely *albergue* there and carry on. In my journal I write that it is one of the hardest walks, asphalt all the way; but curiously on my Michelin map I have written clearly: *very beautiful road, lovely walk*. I am baffled now, and, search my memory as I might, I am unable to remember one single step past Murias. Perhaps this was where I slipped down the rabbit hole ... It is the hottest day, high 20's, I water myself as I walk and pause to pour three or four drops on my rose companion of the day which I find, pick, and tuck into my chest strap. The snow on the mountains seems close.

I reach Rabanal just before the *albergue* is open and wait with a young Italian who is in severe pain. Gaucelmo is owned by the English Confraternity of St James and here in this foreign field is the perfect 'forever England'. Herb gardens, old walls with roses tumbling over, an acre or so of grass with un-mown circles of wild meadow under the silver birches, the kindly familiarity of queues and the promise of tea at four o'clock. Susanna welcomes me. She is, though at that moment I am unaware of this singular synchronicity, the closest friend of Maria McCann, Glastonbury novelist and neighbour. Could I invent all these connections even if I tried? No. They defy logic. I love being barefoot on soft English grass (did someone bring the seed over?), love the drone of bees in the clover – and learn that tonight Dane is playing in the 12th century church just opposite. When I walk over to the church later there in front of me is the Frenchman in the wheelchair.

Meeting each of these two men, Dane and Didier, adds an extra dimension to my day.

16

Wild Dogs, Wheelchairs and an Unlikely Banana!

Rabanal is a minute hamlet. I buy food at Miriams, come back to the *albergue* and make a healthy bowl of provisions, am not allowed a dribble of olive oil, but given a bottle of cooking oil by one of the two male *hospitaleros*. I sit at the al fresco table where the two male *hospitaleros* and the real olive oil sits and dress my salad with it when the men are pre-occupied with ogling young *peregrinas;* just *because.* Then I learn of cold showers – the plumbers have been working all day. Regardless, I wash Everything and me, hang my clothes on the long lines in the hot sun. I love being here on English grass with bare feet and clover and patches of wild flowers under the silver birches. The garden is a blessed sanctuary. Susanna is a delight – the two men ... ah well. At lunch I had tried to lead the table talk but it fell away in trifles and though I may have missed the currant cake I couldn't help but notice the undercurrents. The Australian is a far cry from enlightenment! A fulsome Philistine, he disparages Dane, whom he hasn't met, Dane is staying at a different *albergue*, his cello, and the entire canon of classical music. Dane's fame travels before him, he is playing in the old 11th century church tonight. The Australian was equally disparaging of the kindness of Marion of the CSJ too – *she* doesn't make the rules, *she's* not a *hospitalera*, it's nothing to do with *her*, his gravel voice grates in response to learning of my original email to her. I just may pass that on.

A little back-story:

When I was panic-planning my walk at 4.00 o'clock in the mornings BC, Before Camino, I had emailed the Confraternity over their inflexible ruling that no pilgrim will be permitted refuge who has not walked and carried his or her pack up that 20 km hill. Now, my feet have a history and so I wrote to the CSJ that their rule was fine for a twenty year old male, but not for a nearly-seventy-year-old woman who had been in a wheelchair and told she would not walk again. The one size rule really doesn't fit all.

Some years back, when I lived in S.E. Queensland, I had tripped on the bottom stair of my verandah – and both feet had crumbled. Just like that. The verdict of the Australian medical fraternity who viewed the collapse of both my feet from such severe osteoporosis was rank dismissal – it was wheelchair for me. No physio was offered, no options except wheelchair – forever. Up till that moment osteoporosis had not been detected – although, at around the same time, I had a tooth removed and a piece of honeycombed jawbone came with it. It puzzled me, but the negligent dentist of the day didn't actually enlighten me as to why half a honeycombed jawbone would have come out attached to the tooth, a tooth which showed no signs of decay.

But back to my foot story: a chance reading of a local newspaper during my months of bed confinement drew my attention to the arrival of a Chinese physiotherapist who set up practice at the bottom of my street. Australia is a Very Large Continent. The bottom of my street isn't mentioned on the maps. Yet Homer Lam came to the bottom of my street. Mark this for a miracle. *Something* demanded I make an appointment to visit him. There is nothing so sad as lying listening to the silent sound of bones crumbling. I was wheeled down to his clinic. Four months had passed since I had been dismissed by the worthy members of the AMA. When Homer opened the door he took one look at my feet, the left one was now an unpretty mottled blue to the ankle, and said gaily: *oh, you have Sudeck's Atrophy, I think I can help you.* And so he did. How he did is a long story of three times weekly visits for nearly a year. What he did is yet another long story, and not for here.

It took nearly four years for me to be able to walk without thinking how to place my foot over, say, a sand ripple or a tussock of grass, anything that required the foot to bend itself. I had to retrain my cellular memory, the cells of my feet, in *how* to walk by thinking for them. I can walk more or less without thinking over any terrain nowadays, but I am still cautious over uneven and serious rockiness underfoot, thinking each footfall in that nanosecond before making it.

The miracle of Homer coming to the bottom of my street is amplified when I tell you that this young man, he was 32 at the time, had a clinic in Hong Kong specializing in Atrophy. Why? you might ask. And I confess I didn't ask. However, logic and a little historical fact suggests to me that with their centuries-long history of foot binding and shattering bones to do so, Chinese women of older generations were/are still susceptible to osteoporosis in their ancestrally weak foot bones. Foot bones are fragile and thin at the best of times. Is it a possibility that it might be some generations *après* footbinding before the inherent and intentional weakness would have bred itself out?

Homer had applied to three universities for post doctoral studies: one in America, one in Canada and one in Australia – St Lucia, in Brisbane. St Lucia answered him first, offering what he wanted. Brisbane is at least 40 kilometres from where I lived in Silkstone, probably more. Imagine 40 kilometres as a radius point from Brisbane. Now swing your mental compass in a huge circumferential arc and you will have a vast area of urban possibilities in which to set up clinic, particularly as he lived in another suburb of Brisbane a long way from Silkstone. Enough said. That he specializes in the very thing that confounded the AMA medics and rendered them incapable of helping me is simply jaw-dropping don't you think? I call all the imponderables that make up my meeting Homer, a miracle. I phoned him BC to ask if he thought I could walk 500 miles with my feet. *Of course you can*, he phoned back, *only you, your feet will do well*. I suspect when my feet reach Santiago, having carried overweight me and overweight *mochila,* they will be stronger than they have ever been in their whole life.

Thus, I emailed Marion to suggest that rules of one size do not fit all. I had nightmares of struggling to reach 'home' and mother-tongue and soft green grass and tea on the lawn and being turned away because I may have resorted to Jacotrans. Marion responded by emailing the *hospitaleros* to alert them to my coming and asking to let me stay. Susanna welcomed me, to my delight and her congratulations I had indeed carried my *mochila* all the 20 kilometres. But, and now I return to the present, this rabid little Australian would have had no compunction in turning me away from my mother-community had I not fitted *his* rule book and arrived sans *mochila* on my back...

I mull over his ungraciousness for three minutes before ditching the thought; the garden and the roses and the old stones in all their loveliness redeem all.

Tea on the lawn at 4.30 but no cucumber sandwiches – ah! English standards are slipping. I've been to vespers. The remarkable Frenchman in the wheelchair is there, his hands black from the rubber wheels and blue with bruising. What courage and determination... He stays for Dane's gorgeous concert, and later I sleep with music in my ears.

A steep climb tomorrow, 1500 metres – 4500 plus feet – to Cruz de Ferro. I can hardly believe I am here. I can lay down Joe's rock at last. He walked the Camino last year, and asked me to carry a rock from his garden in Glastonbury to place with the millions of others at the Cruz de Ferro, with prayers for his family and prayers for England. I have carried it all the way!

To Acebo: 12th June 2014

The day had unfolded with its share of magic. Breakfast at Gaucelmo with very good coffee, jam and bread. I had a yoghurt bought yesterday from the shop. Susanna and Michael, the other English *hospitalero*, ask after my feet and Susanna will email Marion to tell her my progress.

I load up and step out into a heavenly morning on a path of wild flowers and dog roses that rapidly turn to heathers and furze as I climbed up through pines and broom higher than me. Dane, Angel, Nancy and Vern are ahead, dappled by light and shade as they climb higher and higher. They did not stay at Gaucelmo; its queues and rules are not comfortable for everyone.

Last night in the dorm Peter Paul told me his sad story. He decided to begin his walk from his front door in Holland on 17th March. He was beginning to feel very much as if he couldn't go on, his legs were in a lot of pain. *Ah*, I said, now beneficiary to Camino wisdom, *you need potassium and magnesium*. He was not taking it. I gave him one of my fizz in a glass tablets to take now and one for the morning; made him promise to take care of himself, to buy some at the next pharmacy.

In the pilgrim box at Gaucelmo was a tube of French miracle NOK! I snaffled it at once. What a gift.

I haven't looked at my map for days, have just been walking until I have had enough, usually fifteen or twenty kilometres, so to come upon the infamous Foncebadón was a delightful surprise. Foncebadón held horrors for Shirley MacLaine, she conjured up the legendary wild dogs to terrify her. True to the urban myth there is a wild dog vast and somnolent in the long grass verge of Foncebadón. It is the size of a small bear and sighs in sheer boredom when I go to take the photo of the Last of the Wild. Foncebadón is also the last *sello* of my first *credencial.*

Next – the Cruz de Ferro, rising to 1504 metres at the Cruz. On and on and up and up, Mercedes is ahead of me tripping along and singing to herself. Such a pretty girl she is. I come to a junction with the main road and I hear a loud whooshing sound increasing in volume. I stop, and just as well, suddenly in front of me whooshes Didier in his wheelchair laughing ecstatically as he free-wheels downhill, phone set to video. It is such a joyful moment to witness. Walking over the hill comes Peter Paul and a Fellow Pilgrim, Didier's temporary helpers. Didier stops in a natural halt in the hollow, spins round and replays his video to P.P. and F.P. to the sound of much laughter. Peter Paul appears a changed man, life is with him.

I cross the road to the white dusty path and continue to climb. On and on, higher and hotter. The mountains loom, snow capped, the valleys deep and green and dappled with chestnut coloured cattle wearing deep toned cow bells; goldfinches and heathers of all kinds.

Suddenly, Cruz de Ferro – and a battalion of one hundred bikies on serious bikes. They spend an hour posing manfully, muscles flexing and tight bike pants bulging, on the mound of rocks at the foot of the Cross. Prayer is not one of their poses. I chuckle to myself. There, by contrast, across the way sits Seamus doing ten decades of the Rosary!

I sit on the opposite bank and have a small picnic in the shade, Joe's rock at the ready. Eventually there is quiet at the Cross and I cross the road, climb up and place Joe's rock, adding my own prayers too. I spent a reflective hour there.

Angel takes a photo when Nancy fails to click my Nikon – a strange *frisson* of irritation from Nancy when I remark that there *are* no photos. I offer it back to her, I would really like a photo to show to Joe; Angel grabs it from her mother and says, *it's a Nikon mom, it's this easy,* and takes one, two, three, photos just like that.

I walk on. Mercedes is with me as we round the path to the sound of a violin. Didier is concentratedly videoing a white robed young man wearing a tall felt Adept hat sitting on a park bench and playing a violin. The sight is so intimate M. and I stop, step off the noisy gravel path and listen to the magic.

On and on to Manjarin which for years boasted a population of one. I think there are three now. Refreshments, flags of all nations, signposts to everywhere, a dog, a shrine, all jostle for attention. Angel sits at a table and feeds a cat. After Manjarin I walk on and up the Collado de las Antenas to 1515 metres.

On the highest plateau, on top of this beautiful world I am walking through, amongst heathers of every shade, lies the most perfect – *banana!* It seems so deliberately placed, so perfectly ripe, I laugh and accept it as a gift; a potassium hit! I am quite alone, the panorama of 360 degrees confirms my solitude. I climb on and on, my heart is singing at the sheer beauty around me. The path now sparkles with quartz crystal, giving a high energy charge to my feet and to my walking. It is a land of heart-stopping beauty. In the heather further on sits Sue and her friend, sharing their picnic. She celebrates her seventieth birthday. Or is it seventy-one. She is very fit! The path is one of the most difficult, uneven, narrow, ascents and descents seem endless. Hours pass. Then, down in a valley – El Acebo!

and the tale continues ...

17

A Couple of Saints and Squirrel Nutkin

Acebo proves a very hard walk on shale, protruding vertical bedrock, many climbs, very high, on and on and on. It was quite hard. Really. And the second hot day, high twenties. I arrive at Acebo at five minutes to two, am the first to stop at the lovely restored *albergue* of San Apóstal Santiago, by the abandoned church on the way out of the hamlet.

It takes a while to reach the tiny hamlet and I follow a pilgrim down through a cutting to the lower path to arrive to find a pretty hamlet where other pilgrims crowd the first *albergues* and the bars. I continue almost to the end of the village and stop. Pedro lets me in. I choose a bunk next to a window, boots and *mochilas* must be left downstairs. A notice says: *First! Have a shower!* And so I do. Hot water, with separate facilities for women and men – bliss.

Apóstol Santiago is charming. Pine cathedral ceilings, spotlessly clean old timber floors and the promise of an evening meal and breakfast. After showering I sit by the roses on an old stone wall. The stones are cool under me, I have been walking for five hours over two mountains in temperatures of high 20's. I find somewhere to eat and choose trout stuffed with ham, eat my ambrosial nectarines later.

Korean pilgrims pass by, terrified of the sun's rays on their skin, they are dressed in sub-arctic wear. Last night in the dorm one Korean tried to shut the window closest to me. *No!* I say, *leave that window open! We are twenty two people in this room and we need fresh air.* *"Open?"* he quivered, *"all night?"* And he donned his arctic wear to wear in bed! At dinner last night he had told us the temperature would reach 40 C today – as he zipped up his thermal jacket. Michael took one look and burst out laughing.

No one is in the bunk above me but it seems everyone else in the *albergue* is hunching up to my end of the three dormettes because they've all experienced another Korean as a killer snorer. This pilgrim has been left in a roomette on his own because of it! There are only eight of us and beds for twenty-three. I would have been alone but for the snorer... Oh well. No one in my section snored – but sod's law prevails. I climb up to the top bunk as no one was above me and lay by the open window, a deep structure set in the two foot thick stone walls, to catch the breeze and have a moon bath. I don't need earplugs until – oh the cats! I lay listening to the huge new timbers of the old house creak and crackle and settle in the cool night air – and then the cats howl. Like banshees they are, gathering from all quarters of the village, right under my window which is covered with stiff wire mosquito netting so I can't pour my water out on to them. I confess howling cats under the window or on hot tin roofs are more than even the most dedicated feline *aficionada* like me can bear. Meanwhile the Korean snores on in the first roomette, counterpoint to the cats' descant.

Breakfast is a bowl of hot milk, or coffee, and a slice of bread and jam. Last night's dinner was a bowl of spaghetti unrelieved by sauce... glad I lunched well.

So I leave Acebo, noting a photo on the wall that shows it completely under snow during winter – no Camino then. It is a very picturesque place. On I walk to Riego de Ambros, a gingerbread village of tumbling old cottages and roses and the road disappears where the yellow arrow points me right and then left. There is no path. I look somewhat aghast at the river bed, the yellow arrow is directing me down this raw river bedrock. It is perilous. I descend foot by inching foot, suddenly conscious of my feet and their history. Goodness I don't want to fall here – it is a hidden place and I am alone. I walk with my walking stick propping me, placing my feet sideways on the steep rocks. I slip, all goes flying, and the weight of my *mochila* hurtles me into the high banks of broom and brushwood. I manage to get up, pick up the walking stick and burst out laughing at the irony of everything – mostly the walking stick story. Willa's walking stick – and therein hangs a tale to tell at the end of my Camino. I shake it heavenwards laughing as I thank her for being *such* a bitch that I now have her walking stick and it has saved my fall!

I continue down, down, down this dramatic and dangerous descent with no views and no end in sight until at last the narrow river bed opens out to wider softer earth. The scent of fox, and I startle a mole running blind to find his hole. It is the third or fourth mole I have seen along the Way, scurrying blind to find its home.

A café in a field – welcome sight. A very rude NZ man arrives demanding coffee, hot toast – *I said hot toast* – he snarls – *with butter, now,* as the pretty, lone, young woman was making my scrambled eggs and coffee. A vulgar queue jumper, he was oblivious to me, the young woman, and the scenario. I said *excuse me...* attempting to salvage both my scrambled eggs and the young woman's confusion – she dropped everything at his rude demands – and the man turns and tells me I should relax and enjoy the Camino experience. His sort beggars belief.

Ponferrada. I'd only walked sixteen kilometres but such a difficult walk made me ache all over, I had descended one thousand metres, and Ponferrada was boiling at 36 C. There were no hotel rooms to be had. I sit in the foyer of one and cry with exhaustion. The kind receptionist gives me two glasses of water and phones the *albergue* which I couldn't find.

Yes, plenty of room, they tell her, though I dread another dorm and sleepless night.

On I walk to the splendid Saint Nicolas de Flue. We queue in the foyer by a fountain for tired feet, some pilgrims are sitting on its wall doing a thing so sensible that I wrestle with myself for not being able to do the same – dangle my hot feet in the cold water while reading a book or chatting... I'm *so* not good in crowds and am too shy to follow suit! The *hospitalero* takes me to a room of four where I am given a bottom bunk – the small wing was for women; marvellous. And Nicolas de Flue? He was a Swiss saint circa 1400 honoured by Catholics and Protestants for the permanent national unity of Switzerland; apparently he survived for nineteen years with no food other than the Eucharist. A farmer, he was illiterate, and a visionary of considerable insight. I send up a prayer of gratitude – this is a grand *albergue*, with good facilities.

In comes Martine, a Frenchwoman. She is in much the same state as I, exhausted and momentarily tearful. She is 65, has walked from Arles, with knees. From *Arles!* A mere 1450 kilometres, no wonder her knees are complaining. Showers do wonders for both of us and off we go to find sustenance. She joyously splashes her face in the cool water of a street fountain. We late-lunch together; a gracious man in Restaurant Templarios will offer us a large mixed salad – the restaurant is closed for the afternoon and the chef has gone home but we can see he pities us women-of-a-certain-age. An American woman follows us in, sits with us, and demands x y z from the menu. We, embarrassed because she appears to be with us, tell her the restaurant is closed and the owner is graciously giving us not a menu but a mixed salad, eat it or don't. She demands from him, he looks puzzled, repeats what he can offer, she is rude, and she gets up and leaves, she doesn't want to eat any of *that*, she says, looking scornfully at our wonderful salads. Martine says she has met her earlier on the Camino, says she hates pilgrims, *albergues* and much else, only stays in hotels and

110

Martine wonders what the Camino will teach her. Grace isn't one of the lessons to date.

I am taken with the castle, though I prefer old monasteries, but once more I am particularly charmed by the public sculpture. A vast wisteria spreading along whole blocks of old houses is supported by an ingenious series of bronze sculpted 'roots' from its span to the ground. I am impressed by the imagination and by the generosity of public funding to allow its creation.

14th June to Villafranca – the hottest day, the worst day and a 24 km walk.

The ugly man from NZ walks ahead of me as I leave Ponferrada. Actually he is a good looking man, but like many of his type was obviously told so by his mother and the demands he makes on the world to fall at *his* feet can likely be laid at *her* feet. How many good looking men have been thus ruined! His wife is limping and I soon pass them along the pretty river walk. He quips: *iggs ind baycon this morning thin?* And I respond lightly with: *not if you're queue-jumping again* which sets his face in stone. I ask his wife about her knee. She is quite unaware of her husband's rudeness of yesterday. She and I chat merrily, take a couple of photos of a painting of Our Lady of Compostela on the outside of a church, while pretty boy fumes. I smile; I can be *cruel!*

The air is filled with the intoxicatingly heady scent of long avenues of flowering *tilleul*, linden, lifting my residual tiredness left over from another disturbed night's sleep. No snoring, but our windows opened on to a bus stop on the street and the full moon brought forth the sleepless of Ponferrada to gather there and discuss how to develop their Templar Castle into a theme park – or something. Then, suddenly, to my surprise and delight, I notice a red squirrel ripple down a tree trunk. I see his long ear tufts russet glowing in the dawn light. I photograph and wait, he reaches ground, turns, sits up, crosses his rufus paws across his white bib and I photograph again. Distant and out of focus, but Squirrel Nutkin all the same.

I meet Joy from Wollongong, a town I once lived in, a town D.H. Lawrence once lived in, a town close to the great Royal National Park, Australia's first, and the second in the world, declared protected in 1879. Joy is 75, small, wiry and fit. We have *café con leche*, she gives me a yoghurt which in this heat won't keep, and we walk a while together. Further on we stop at a cool way-stop under trees with plenty of water, I wet my scarf and drape it over my shoulders before I trudge on to Villafranca. The bitumen of this stretch of road reflects its heat back to me and, though I do not yet know it, the temperature will reach 36 C by 6 o'clock this evening. I am struggling. The church *albergue* of Cacabelos looks marvellous, I have marked it in my Michelin for its recommendations, but it is too early for it to open and I decide to continue on to Villafranca del Bierzo.

The trail of pilgrims shows us all suffering along this stretch. A hill looms ahead, I attempt to hitch hike. Of course no one stops; other pilgrims are doing the same! It is an endlessly weary asphalt walk with little shade – I have seven kilometres to go. There is no sign of the town, not at all. Then down steep cobbled lanes to outdo Clovelly there is – Villafranca. But something terrible happens to my eyes – they are stinging, tears are streaming down my face and I cannot see. I cannot see at all! I'd wet my scarf and so wash my eyes – it is horrible, I simply cannot see. My feet are cramping and my heel feels bruised – I lurch into a human, a young Spanish man as it happens, and he takes me by the arm down the steep cobbles, slowly, and with great concern leads me to the doors of Hotel San Francisco. He leaves, and the receptionist leads me upstairs to a room. My eyes burn like coals and my legs are rigid. Even stretching, which I mostly forget to do, hurts too much. But, no blisters. A shower first, in a bath with a wondrous wide shelf to sit on, and then horizontal. Feet up, legs up, I rue having eaten my cucumber or I'd have put slices of it on my eyes. I cannot open my eyes, but I rest in the bliss of cool cotton sheets, a breeze from the balcony and I decide to stay two nights. My hair is silently turning greyer by the minute, must be in protest at the shock to my body of doing half marathons at my unfit age.

The significance of San Francisco, Saint Francis, will slowly dawn on me. There are no accidents.

18

Rest, Reflections and a Revelation in Villafranca del Bierzo

Hours later hunger compels me to dress and look for food. I am thoroughly taken in by a touting restaurateur and led down into a dungeon off the main square. The square is bright and full of happily dining people, why don't I stay and eat here? But it is a weak moment and I am now semi-blind, my eyes hurt, my legs hurt, I suppose I want to be cared for, coddled, and not have to make a decision as to where to eat. I order, but am given mussels not mushrooms, the main course is a mediocre something, and I am overcharged on my debit card by a rather large amount, fifty percent in fact, but I am too blind and cramped to register it until back in my hotel and horizontal. Once home in my room I lay on my bed, dealing mentally with the man, too unwell to go back and right the wrong. As the only deliberately negative experience along the entire Camino I decide to let it be. I can't even recall the name of the place to shame him in print forever.

At night the 36 C drops to 8 C and the radiators go on. I am cosy and warm, and welcome the thick blankets which I had earlier pulled off. In the morning my eyes are normal and I watch pilgrims going spritely down the street, but I will stay another day, let my legs return to normal. I buy organic kefir and peaches, full, sweet and dripping with juice, the like of which I haven't tasted in decades – these have been allowed to live out their allotted span to reach perfection on their trees in the sun. Cherries I still have from the trees along the way, and I add a delicious organic gazpacho soup to my purchases, made by, so the packet tells me, Saint Teresa. The little grocery store on the corner of the plaza has everything delicious and I indulge in the breads and cheeses too. It is owned by a woman who seems to care much for her produce...

As I cross the plaza I meet the cheating restaurateur – he has the grace to squirm under my gaze and scuttles down the lane back to his dungeon! Why! I think, not entirely surprised at his rapid disappearance, he *knew* what he was up to and guilt has caught him. I'll bet he thought I'd be gone in the morning with every other one-night-pilgrim who passes through Villafranca ... but here I am, standing here as large as his guilt! I'm rather pleased that I didn't return to chide him by quoting Papal Bull, Book and Candle for stealing from a *peregrina*! What did a friend once say: *karma is never cruel but it is uncannily accurate!*

I woke in a low moment actually, one of those moments of self-doubt and feeling – I dislike the word but it suits – *ugly*. Flashes of mother's mantra: *you are fat, you are stupid, you are ugly,* ricochet around my head. Funny how the words surfaces to hit me in the face, so to speak, when faced with a mirror. I console myself with the thought that Pericles apparently felt the same about the shape of his head too, and concealed it for posterity to remember him by always wearing a shining and handsome helmet. We, Pericles and I, share a keen sense of democracy and fair play – small coin for a woman who, when all is said and done, would just love to be pretty and loved. I smile at the comparison and know that I have, at least, a shining and beautiful humour.

Downstairs I meet Ann from Brighton, we had met at Gaucelmo. She stayed last night at Cacabelos for €5 and found the place beautiful, only two beds in each room, she tells me, and the rooms are built in a horseshoe around the church. I felt worse then as I had told myself to stay there, marked it in my Michelin Guide. Walking on to Villafranca cost me my eyes, my legs, and €60 for two nights in San Francisco! A CD of songs by Loreena McKennitt is playing in the café; I share with Ann the breathtaking youtube film by Hikmet Sesinoy, a Chechnyan whose wild mountains, dancing men, fleet-hooved horses, flying hawks and exquisite women, lifts McKennitt's song *Night Ride Across The Caucasus* to a level of pure enchantment. Ann notes it in her diary, will watch it when she gets home. I walk with her to the edge of town, we hug goodbye, she looks at my feet: *they don't look like they've walked any distance at all,* she laughs, *they're beautiful!* I laugh too, *I only told them they were beautiful this very morning,* I respond, as Ann hugs me again and adds, out of the blue, *and you are beautiful too.* I know a shadow passes my face; I nod, tell her I probably needed *just* those words *just* this morning, thank her, and watch as she walks down the pilgrim path and over the bridge. She has chosen to take the mountain path of the three available out of Villafranca.

Following the road I continue to a café for *café con leche,* ponder on how timely things are, how right things just happen when the heart cries. I pass a very large building and glance up, aware of a huge poster hanging on its wall. Something calls me across the road to look up and I strain to read it. Good Heavens! This Revelation is telling me that St Francis was here in 1214, 800 years ago. Is it possible? I didn't know that and I've read much of St Francis and furthermore I spent ten days in Assisi over Christmas and no one told me anything about Saint Francis on the Camino then. Mind you, no one who is Christian knows he spent two years with Sultan Malik al-Kamil either, *not* trying to 'convert' him – really, people are *so* self-congratulatory – but sharing like with like as men of God. Sultan Malik, the nephew of the great Kurd, Saladin, whose exemplary behaviour towards even the worst of the barbarous Crusaders shames us now, was something of a mystic, and great souls recognise each other.

In the time it takes to photograph the poster all these thoughts run through my mind; am I re-tracing footsteps of past lives? I have my own Kurd stories and I ponder on the fact of my being here at all. Am I rounding off karmic circles? Completing things? I've led such a strange life, been so obedient to its inner dictates. In the comfort of my journal I write the story of St Seraphim in his forest: a woodman or someone comes to him for spiritual advice and said *Father Seraphim I can hardly look at you, your face is shining like the sun, the light dazzles me.* Saint Seraphim placed his hands on the man's shoulders and said *you can see me like this because you are lit by the same dazzling light.* As a man is, so he sees. Blake said that about men chopping down trees too. It's almost a commonplace; we see in others what we are, or what we potentially are. Such a comforting thought, one day I'll be nice in spite of Mother's Mantras! I like nice people! And then I remember Father Bede, who stayed with me shortly before he died, telling me I had the consciousness of the Holy, and that I must continue his journey to the Black Madonna for him and for women. These are mighty thoughts for a morning.

I return to the Pilgrim Bridge and photograph the striding stone *peregrino* just as the three Americans arrive. They are such nice men, we meet and pass from time to time but now we stay awhile and talk, they too are having a rest day as one of them suffered from the boiling walk yesterday. Two are walking, the third is unable to and drives a car to meet them at their hotels each evening. They are diplomats, one is based in Paris at the American Embassy, they have walked together many times over the years. They tell me they have ditched their John Brierley – *dreadful book,* say two of them – found the guidebook of Alison Raju and admire her intelligence. We chuckle again and Chris points out the easiest of the three possible roads out for tomorrow. The Dragonet, or is it the Dragonte, is not for me, nor the Camino Duro thank you; their very names are enough to deter a tired *peregrina*.

I wander back to the mediaeval part of town and up to the Door of Pardon, *Puerte de Perdón*, where in days gone by pilgrims who were too ill to continue on to Santiago de *Compostela* would be cleansed of their sins by touching the door. I too touch the door and a great sigh escapes me. I'll deal with my sins later. But for now I think that being here and not in Cacabelos is exactly where I am intended to be or I would not be aware that I am following Saint Francis' footsteps.

19

Bedbugs, Bodhisattvas and A Brave Climb to Contemplate

16ᵗʰ June

I am ready to leave. I lay awake for ages waiting to hear the first pilgrims pass under my balcony from the *albergues* up the street as I have no clock to tell me the hour and don't want to walk in the dark for too long. I finish yesterday with a longish walk around the town and valley, came back to cut toenails and fingernails, wash out Everything, re-pack and have another luxurious bath. I sleep wondrously.

It is 8 C and 6 a.m. In twelve hours it will be 36 C. Today I am off to Vega and Ruitelán, 20 kilometres, all trees and shade, a flat road and a river running alongside. It is a beautiful walk along the N6; cherries hang well in reach as I pass laden trees and fill a small bag. Yet this walk has suffered another of John Brierley's denouncements and dire warnings not to travel it. Really that man! When did he last walk the Camino? Check for accuracy? Wake up and get real? Update his guide book? Telling tired pilgrims to walk the Dragonte or the Duro because he thinks these paths 'more spiritual' really is the limit! Bitumen, according to JB who enjoys a good car that needs bitumen, is not spiritual. Really? What of the birds, the trees, the ease of walking, the cherries, the river, the riversong, the coolness, the sheer pleasure of not having to puff and pant and lug one's *mochila* up and down unendurable hills? All this wonder of the walk along the N6, decommissioned as a main arterial since the new motorway flyover bypasses it, inclines one to pleasant thoughts, even spiritual thoughts. I wonder what's a 'spiritual' thought anyway? Thinking about murdering a snorer or two is *most* restorative for *my* spirits!

And so I do walk along the N6 the whole way, it is under massive trees, serenaded with birdsong and the river runs alongside. The river, the day's other alphabet, murmuring from every ripple glimpsed through dense foliage, singing round every boulder, shimmering pink and dark slate from every reflection charms me. I don't find I'm thinking much at all. Only two cars, Guardia Civil on a routine drive, pass me during the entire walk of many hours until at least the village of Vega de Valcarce, which is tiny and certainly not the stuff of spaghetti junctions. All traffic has been re-routed along the triple by-pass of an autobahn hundreds of feet above this green and forested part of the Camino. I catch glimpses of these soaring highways as the river valley road rounds its bends. Four military men, their dog and a colourful flag, pass me in Trabadelo. I understand them to be helicopter pilots in the army, from the Basque country, but understanding in a language I don't speak has moveable goal posts. They are *peregrinos*, off to Santiago de Compostela, a gay sight indeed.

Foxgloves line the banks. Ambasmestas has great coffee, strong and full-flavoured, *organic* says the barman who takes the most infinite pains to slice Serrano ham and Manchego cheese to make a *bocadilla* for my journey. Vega del Valcarce is so tidy, like the spa town of Alet-le-Bains, probably with a similar population count reaching – three figures! I continue to Ruitelán, population, 11?

I wait in the rose trellised courtyard garden of the Pequeño Potala. Their clothes washing sink is outside so I wash my socks and hang them on the lines. Registration will open at midday, not long to wait. It is run on military lines by two men who may be more than friends. In my journal I write: *run by a neurotic pair of pansies.* One of them barks: *Close the windows! Flies! No Jacotrans now! Put All credencials here! Do not go out* this *door, come in only, and only once! Go out* that *door! And ALL pilgrims will eat together at 7.30.*

I demur at the last injunction, preferring not to eat late meals when I go so early to bed – to no avail. Instructions are delivered with the terrific power of a Cerberus barking at the Gates of the Underworld. I accept the reasons but find the staccato machine gun delivery hard to bear after a 20 kilometres walk with nothing more disturbing than birdsong and wind in the trees. It is a large judgement to make on two men I do not know and I am happy to be proved too hasty a few minutes later when another side to the military manners shines through.

In came a boy with bedbugs. He had come from Villafranca, from *albergue* Refugio Ave Fénix which has a reputation for a distinct lack of hygiene since Jesus Jato died. Carlos brought the boy outside to the rose terraces and gave him three huge plastic sacks to empty his belongings into and a set of clean clothes to wear after his shower. Everything will be frozen overnight in a huge ice-cream deep freezer over in the neighbouring hotel! Freezing kills bedbugs. Other *albergues* may well have turned away the Danish boy, but here in Pequeño Potala he is kindly received. Bedbugs are the scourge of all the *refugios* and hostels from St Jean Pied de Port to Finisterre; bedbugs are taken very seriously along the Way, and *refugios* can be closed for weeks during fumigation of an infestation. Bedbugs are carried by pilgrims from one *refugio* to another. Celi translates this as I see the huge red weals of bedbug bites covering the boy's back and arms. I observe kindness and compassion now flow freely in this little Potala, a far cry from the peremptory welcome of an hour before.

17th June

As quite the Cat Who Walks by Herself I find the loud *bonhomie* of strangers around the dinner table uncomfortable. I recognize my misalignment to the human race, know that hermits in pairs are more my line. Like any good feline I sit quietly and neatly at the table, paws folded, closest to the food, a vast tureen of cream of carrot soup made from locally grown carrots. Carlos asks me to serve it to all, perhaps sensing in me the truer comfort zone of *doing* something. The meal that follows is superb, and all vegetarian. The cacophony around me makes it easy to silently pay homage to this splendid meal. Later, a good night's sleep in a small dorm with three other women, no snorers, windows wide open. At 6.30 a pop style rendering of Gounod's Ave Maria wakes us, it would waken the dead, and we are invited to a marvellous breakfast of hot milk, muesli, real coffee, toast, rolls, jams, honey, boiled eggs, teas of all kind ... as much as one needed. How do these two men do it day after day, night after night, year after year and all for €15? Little Bodhisattvas of Pequeño Potala, *thank you!*

Today I face the one stretch of the whole Camino over which I have serious qualms. I doubt about being able to climb – O Cebreiro. It is only a ten kilometres walk but nine and a half of those kilometres are vertical. I will climb 700 metres, that's over 2000 feet, to reach 5000 feet above sea level. These seem incredible statistics for someone who lives at sea level on the Somerset Levels! I will give it a go. I'm glad I left instructions for my Requiem Mass with Father James – just in case. I have passed so many crosses of pilgrims who died on the Camino I fully expect this climb to O Cebreiro to be the last time I put one foot in front of another on planet Earth. One step at a time and don't look up, I remind myself. I check the Jacotrans label on my *mochila* one last time, tie my boots firmly, pick up my stick and, Gathering All My Determination, bid my farewells.

20

O Cebreiro! O Epiphany!

I left at 7 o'clock, in 8 degrees Celsius. I record now that it reached high 20's in high O Cebreiro. The path was comfortable for some while; crumbly asphalt wound through tiny hamlets, a number of which offered horse riding as an alternative to walking the mountain to O Cebreiro. I thought it a wondrous idea, but the notices proved carrots, always leading on to the next notice and promise and then the next – until I suspect one's belief in their actually being any horses to ride ends up making one feel a complete ass!

After Las Herrerias the path took on a different character altogether. Now I was struggling with the ascent and the rocks and the slippery boulders as a whole lot of pilgrims attempted to jostle past me on the narrow defile. There was a considerable drop on my right, over which I did not want to hurtle, and I held my place along the ascent with difficulty as faster pilgrims assumed a sense of entitlement. I waited, immovable, while they changed to Indian file and passed me. This same sense of entitlement astonishes me on high-hedged English country lanes too when cyclists blithely ride two or three abreast with no thought under their silly helmets of the possibility of sharing the narrow lanes. There'd be a few less swipes in their direction from irritated motorists banked up behind them in second gear if *they* went single file. I couldn't safely go any faster, stood my ground, and bore the frowns. Going single file through the defile interrupted their conversations!

At last the remaining morning rush of pilgrims from Vega and Ruitelán disappeared ahead of me and I could continue at my own pace, plodding along, stopping for breath every few minutes. It was fairly dense but open-leaved forest here, no views but the rocks underfoot. On and on I went climbing and climbing, climbing all the time, 630 metres to 1330 metres, only looking back down, not up or forward, when I pause. It was more than an effort and time seemed very slow in responding to my getting anywhere at all. In due time I came out of deep forest and could see a couple of farm buildings with an arrow pointing straight and an arrow pointing right and saying *Albergue de La Faba*. I went right, anything to break the intensity of the climb.

I am so glad I did. I came to an eleventh century church and an *albergue* of exquisiteness and there in the courtyard stands that most famous of all famous pilgrim statues of an old wild bearded man striding into the wind, his sandals slapping the earth. It was an enchanted space. Pilgrims had already left and the *hospitalero* spent a few minutes talking to me of the history of the *albergue* of la Faba. Try as I might I cannot recall the name of the princess who commissioned the statue – Fürstenberg? Württemburg? – my memory has hitched itself to a passing cloud.

The pause refreshes me; I look at my guide profile, pretty impressive I reckon. Another 300 vertical metres to La Laguna ... But now the scenery changes dramatically, I am on top of the mountains and the views unfold as I walk. I see huge quartz crystals on farm gateposts, on roofs of houses, on old cattle sheds, purposefully placed. A young man came out from an impressive house just as I am contemplating his climbing roses and believing the sign that comforts me with *O Cebreiro 4 kilometres* and I ask him why the crystals? I am not at all surprised when he says, surprised that I would need to ask such an obvious question: *they bring down the light, conduct energies.* Earth wisdom here is not confined to esoteric books in the

High Street, it is a genetic inheritance. El Acebo and La Faba are quite my favourite secrets.

The road to O Cebreiro seems easy now; the quartz underfoot really does impart a charge. I remember the first time I set foot on Magnetic Island I was dizzy for two whole days, quite discombobulated. I couldn't shake the feeling off but on the third day it disappeared, my head cleared, and I've never had the experience there since. The instruments of Captain Cook's ship went haywire when he came close to the island, hence his naming it Magnetic. The island is granite, and granite is a natural source of radiation; the granite on Maggie Island has huge amounts of quartz and walking on the island gives the same feeling of 'bounce'. I am frequently amazed at how similar parts of the Spain I have walked through are to parts of the Australia I love.

Now I leave the village of La Faba the hills roll away from the eye, range on range, silhouettes of lilac, mauve, smoke. With a pang of nostalgia they remind me of looking out over the valleys of Numinbah, Beechmont, Lamington, Binna Burra, Springbrook, beloved mountains, ancient escarpments, perhaps not so high, of the Great Dividing Range of southern Queensland. I dawdle, entranced, all feeling of effort suspended.

I once had a dentist in Exmouth who disappeared for three weeks every year to walk. One day I asked him where he went. At that time walk for me was a four letter word; it was curiosity that prompted the question. *You won't know it*, he said, *it's the most beautiful place in the world and it's in Australia. Try me*, I replied and he said: *Springbrook*. I laughed and said, *you're right, it is paradise, and I've a block of land up there near Purlingbrook Falls!* My book, *Patrick and the Cat Who Saw beyond Time*, is set right there on that magical plateau of mists and waterfalls, lookouts and spectacular bird life.

My reveries have brought me to La Laguna, the road is easy, winding up and up and beautiful beyond words. Close to what I think must the top, well past La Laguna, I turn to grasp the magnitude of the 360 degree view and see just behind me the two Japanese legends I have heard other pilgrims speak of. They are seventy-nine and eighty-one, or is it eighty-nine and ninety-one? At their great age it's almost academic. They seem tiny, slender, fragile figures as they hug the edge of the path coming to one of the crests. Beyond them I count seven mountain ranges, silhouettes fading to azure smoke in the skyline. The scene is almost unearthly in its beauty and burns itself into my heart. The Japanese couple are doing the whole Camino. *Precious*, I think and offer to take a photo of the pair of them with their camera. They are delighted. Not a word is recognised between us.

Then – Galicia! I have reached the painted monolith that marks the boundary between Castilla y León and Galicia! I have come to the last of the provinces of the whole of northern Spain. It is Galicia all the way now. I am almost sad, I love this adventure in spite of being exhausted and in pain one way or another over much of my poor old bod much of the time! But, no blisters! And I have seen some horrific feet along the Way; many pilgrims are forced to drop out. As I stand at the milestone a young Italian offers to take my photo, and takes a couple of others for good measure with the views all around. Who would believe me without these photos ... I can barely believe it myself. I remember Wolfgang of La Faba telling me Didier made it up in his *wheelchair*, he took the road, not the path of course, and Wolfgang drove him on to O Cebreiro. How privileged I am to be able to walk with these feet, these mountains...

And I enter the village of O Cebreiro. I am charmed by the thatched roofs and round buildings and I imagine winter to be serious here at such heights. Chris is here, he suggests we have a coffee while he waits for his fellow walker and fellow driver.

We learn a little of each other's lives, he loves cats and I am guided by a Ralph Cupboard* sleeping on the window sill of a private house to seek for a room. If I don't find one, says Chris, as all appear full and I won't stay in an *albergue*-of-snores in such a divine place, I can sleep in their car. The three of them have pre-booked hotels all the way.

The lady with the last private room in the village apologizes that it is *pequeño frío*, and by golly it is! But it is ensuite, the bedding would satisfy the princess and the pea it is so thick, the wardrobe is stacked with seven more quilts should I need them, the window is too high to look out of and I think that *may* be a pair of knees walking past. No wonder the room is so cold, it is probably the wine cellar! For my purpose it is perfect, and Ralph Cupboard leans against the external window alcove warming himself in the sun that doesn't quite enter my fridge. Cats along the Camino are not well treated as a rule, I've seen some sad ones along the way, and I stopped a man throwing a stone at a very pregnant and hungry mother cat way back, so to know my hostess has three happy ginger cats is a comfort. An atmosphere charged with cruelty is a hard thing to abide in. The huge key to my room is kept behind a large baroque French enamel and ormolu clock in a niche in the salon wall.

Lunch is a succulent stew, meat, falling of the ribs of a rib cage so generous I wonder if they've unearthed an Auroch or two. I wash it down with a small bottle of dry local cider which is crisp, thirst-quenching and delicious. A quaint tin cut out pilgrim sits by the wall of the hostel whose food is, I learn, also legendary.

Full and happy and so proud of myself for climbing O Cebreiro, which doesn't seem difficult at all now I am here in heaven, I go over to the eighth century church to say thank you – and I am undone ... but the Epiphany and the Holy Grail must wait to be told, for even Ezekiel's response to his bizarre experience was to sit dumbfounded for seven days; a stretch of time proper for digesting a divine vision.

21

O Epiphany! O Holy Grail!

I wander over to the little 8th century church with the intention of saying thank you to the memory of Don Elías Valiña Sampedro the rather saintly priest who painted yellow arrows along the entire Camino from Roncesvalles to Finisterre. And then re-painted them when they needed it. He may have invented the yellow cockleshell milestones too – but whatever he did I am fiercely grateful he did it.

I walk in to the church directly to the left chapel where his grave is. Thank you's said, I glance up to see a statue of St Benedict. Father Bede made me an Oblate of St Benedict years ago in Shantivanam. St Benedict and St Francis appeal to me for being just laymen seeking holiness. Not piety, which is pretentious, but holiness, wholeness, an integrity of living. I smile, and wander over to the other side chapel where, on the wall, is a splendid 11th century Virgin in Majesty. There she sits, on her Throne of Wisdom, *le Trône de la Sagesse,* just as she should. Seeing her catapults my thoughts back to my research throughout France in the late nineties tracking down these wonderful images in response to Father Bede's request that I do so, for him and for women. I count my blessings: two great mystics have each taken me under their wings before I had wings of my own with which to fly: Father Bede and Mrs Tweedie. Remembering what *she* told me of the timeless links in the Chain of Succession brings a prickle of tears to my eyes as I stand there. The church seems incredibly warm suddenly, as if I am cocooned in a warmth not quite actual.

I look to my left. There are people sitting and praying or simply gazing at an alcove in which is a glass cabinet displaying a patten, a chalice and two cruets. I blink and go closer. I can't read Spanish but I do know the meaning of San Graal – a grail, "wondrous but not explicitly holy" and connected to the Arthurian legends but even more essentially to Joseph of Arimathea. What's *he* doing here? I think, surprised. The Glastonbury legend tells us Joseph of Arimathea came *there* after the Crucifixion, carrying *two cruets* which contained the blood and sweat of Christ... Goosebumps add to the prickling sensation I am experiencing, and with it a sense of dislocation. These things – St Benedict, Mary in Majesty, two cruets and a chalice said to be the Holy Grail – are powerful mnemonics of remembrance Past, almost Far Memory stuff. All in one tiny church.

I decide to leave, to ground myself with a hot chocolate after such an exertion of climbing. I don't reach the door. On my right is a small side chapel and ever curious I go in – and I am undone. In this empty, holy, place is a copy of the Cross of San Damiano, the Cross ever linked to St Francis. Unbidden, tears flow down my face. I cry, these stones ... this remembrance ... I am overwhelmed by a flood of images that takes me back to last Christmas when I went for the first time to Assisi...

Assisi – Christmas 2013: on my second day there the fog came down so thickly no one but me ventured out. I was alone. The fog was so thick I struggled to see my hand at the end of my arm. Santa Chiara, a vast, vast Cathedral, was completely invisible as I stood in the piazza by the fountain in front of it. The fog was a white and silent duvet over the whole of Assisi but I couldn't bear to waste time by staying in my room. I ended up walking, climbing, a long winding road right out of the fog to the Eremi, the Hermitage. It was a blessed choice. A hoopoe flew overhead as I walked. Farmlets were named Upupe, the Italian name for this pretty bird whose presence on other pilgrimages of mine highlit, for me, significant rites of passage. A decade beforehand I had painted an icon of St Francis *with a hoopoe* – how could I have known then of its place in *his* forest?

Up at the Hermitage I was above the fog-line. Looking down I could see only a dense white blanket without even a church spire to suggest Assisi might still be there. More than foolish, I decided to take a path down through the forest from the Hermitage, my rationale being that it would be shorter than the long winding road; and in equal measure, it would have been the path St Francis walked. The fog had time-travelled me back 800 years. Footfall by silent footfall I inched down through the forest in the fog guided only by keening my ears to the quarter-hourly sound of church bells far below me.

The day before the fog came down, in the Cathedral of Santa Chiara, I found the Cross of San Damiano. It is fundamental to the whole exegesis of the man who wrote the Canticle to Creation; surely the first Code for the care of animals and the whole earth. The point of my *divertissement* here is that I went down to the museum in the crypt of the Cathedral and I was floored at the sight of the gown St Clare had made for herself when she left all to follow Francis, who wasn't yet a saint. It was *mine*.

I kid you not. I was even wearing something almost identical at that very moment. I have always worn loose layers, tunics, over-garments, and *this*, this epiphany in front of me, was the prototype. Now, I am no reincarnation of St Clare (or Cleopatra, or Mary Magdalene, she who walks the High Street of Glastonbury in clones, or Morgan le Fée another commonplace clone in Glastonbury), but I swear to you that garment was *mine*. The stone steps to the crypt held my boots fast as I gazed at this mediaeval marvel in its glass cabinet. It was a Goosebump Moment. The garments of St Francis were there too, St Clare had made them all. Slightly dazed, I left the

Cathedral and walked down to San Damiano. A sizzling sensation through the soles of my feet left me in no doubt I was walking in the footsteps of St Francis. It was only a slight suspension of thought, an incline to the left of my current universe, to claim my place in the twelfth century. San Damiano was a different epiphany moment, in this garden St Francis had written his Canticle praising Brother Sun and Sister Moon...

More was to come. I continued to explore this tiny church where St Clare lived for over forty years, fell in love with the fresco of the Madonna above the altar, and was led up very worn stone stairs to come face to face with bronze statue of St Francis and – a *Hare*. Oh my!

A hare, another flood of memories ... the symbols of my own life were coming so thick and fast my brain couldn't travel that way, couldn't keep time.

2012 was my *annus horribilis*. I doubted I would survive it but I did, and its final transition and return to normality was dramatic. One morning, after almost a whole year in a kind of stasis after a minor car crash (not my fault, thank goodness) as the litany of events unfolded, I woke up completely free of their effect after two significant dreams, neither of which were relevant to what came next. I was compelled to paint a *hare*. I did. The painting took me seven days and my revelation of the hare as a once sacred creature then took me to north Wales to the shrine of the Hare and of St Melangell, the 6th century princess turned holy woman for whom the Prince of Powys ceased hunting hares. After my painting of the hare came a painting of a hoopoe. I have never painted animals; I have barely ever painted anything. They came, perfect and exquisite, a kind of blessing from the inner world where symbols sacred to our individual psyche abide. In front of that bronze statue I knew I was in the presence of a mystery, it spoke through me, and it would continue to guide me.

And I haven't even mentioned the synchronicity of my 'chance' meeting with a stranger named Mary in the Queensland Art Gallery in Brisbane who told me over coffee at a shared table in the Gallery café of a book she was reading on the life of St Francis which title lit up a flame of longing that I must go to Assisi...

Now, six months later, I am standing in an 8th century church in Galicia where St Francis has lived.

The girl at the reception desk of the church comes to me, sees how moved I am. *Did you not know this of St Francis?* she asks, *that he walked here, walked the Camino? The Benedictine fathers who built this church gave it to him... For this year you can have two Compostelas, one to commemorate 800 years of St Francis. We have even this credencial ...*

As I ponder all this the dear girl stamps my new *credencial* of St Francis and St James, Santiago. We are both teary. We hug, bound by a common understanding of the magnitude of synchronicities and I go to sit and contemplate all these not-so coincidences over a cup of very hot chocolate. There is yet one more surprise before my day ends.

22

O Holy Grail – O Weston-super-Mare!

I recover my equanimity and walk back to my room. I meet one of the Americans on the way and mention St Francis and the cabinet holding the Grail. Chris is surprised that I hadn't known: there is a huge monolith at the entrance to the village, he tells me, with a bronze of the Grail story. I hurry back to see what I have missed. Sure enough there it is – a bronze map of England and Spain, and a trail marked of the Holy Grail and its journey with Parsifal to O Cebreiro from – *Western-super-Mare!* Wolfram von Eschenbach's story, on *this* map for the world to see, bypasses Glastonbury altogether. Well! Well! is all I can manage as my loyalties are seriously miffed. Even more disagreeable is that this bronze map of Britain in front of *me*, one of Boadicea's daughters no less, doesn't mention Glastonbury at all! My sizzling indignation grows apace! Weston-super-Mare! That mud bound plot – huh! No *way* Weston-super-Mud will ever be named "this holiest Erthe", as Glastonbury is. This is borderline blasphemy to a Glastonbury gal like me and I need another hot chocolate.

I am steeped in these legends, yet I am aware that in no Glastonbury church are these images given concrete form. Joseph of Arimathea appears in the contemporary tapestry behind the altar of St Mary, Our Lady of Glastonbury; the window of St Joseph of Arimathea in St John's is Victorian; Langport has a mediaeval window of St Joseph of Arimathea, but neither Grail nor cruets have ever been found. Did Herr W. von E. know something about Weston-super-Mare that no one else does? Or did the sculptor of the bronze map just fancy the triple barrel name? I ask you, the Holy Grail in *Weston-super-Mare!* Huge billowing laughter rises in me as I stand in front of this grand *non-sequitur* and I stroll across to the knoll, laughing to myself, to wonder at the foolishness of humankind, and myself particularly, for our, my, fierce attachments to our, my, little conceits and vanities.

Later I go to the pilgrim Mass in the church. A woman in her forties or so stands next to me. She shuffles uncomfortably and I glance down. I am appalled at the sight of both her feet which have horrific blisters, are bandaged with transparent elastic weave over the whole foot, pulled over massive pads and gauze bandages all over her heels, toes, balls of her feet. Her pain reaches me. Feeling helpless I send a prayer to Santa María la Real up there on the wall to help heal them.

The priest invites people of different languages to read the Reading. After my earlier epiphany bathos follows. The reading in English is offered by an older American woman with a voice that would grate cheese. Actually it would grate the Cheesewring down on Bodmin Moor. She hasn't the grace to genuflect before stomping up to the lectern either, a sure test for my tired tolerance levels in spite of my restorative laughter of less than an hour before. Her voice is painful to listen to, she relishes her moment with the microphone; her excruciating mispronunciation renders the already ghastly reading of the day incomprehensible, which is probably just as well, it's the Ahab Jezebel scenario.

I happen to have great sympathy for Jezebel. She was related to Dido, the tragic Queen of Carthage whom Aeneas used, abused and betrayed, and so the world lost Carthage. Her Lament from Handel's Xerxes, especially when sung by Dame Janet Baker of the Divine Voice, is quite the most haunting aria I know. Jezebel worshipped Astarte, Ishtar, the Mother Goddess, which is right and proper for a woman to do. The

Jews of the day didn't like *that*. Jezebel was thrown out of a window by the worthies to be eaten by a pack of dogs; *thrown to the dogs*. Our Jezebel was also a Daughter of Zion, an inconvenient truth when it came to getting rid of her. The Hebrews, on the other hand, worshipped female deities, SHE, who was to be later eradicated under the extreme pressure of the male Jewish priesthood. Reflecting on this I forgave the cheese grater for not being able to pronounce what she read, she probably couldn't believe what she was reading!

I squirm. I've never fathomed why we insist on perpetuating the Old Testament when its blatant mal-treatment of women and nature runs counter to the new leaf Jesus was said to have turned. The OT has long been on my list of books to-be-sidelined as antithetical to women.

The priest was lovely. He asked St Francis and St Clare and St James to protect and guide all *peregrinos* safely to Santiago de Compostela.

And so to bed. I fold up one of the seven quilts lengthwise to lay out on the glacial tile floor of my iceberg so I can step warmly all the way to the loo. I eat cake in bed, and spend ages writing.

O Cebreiro has been my epiphany. I leave as the sun is rising. I know my own Camino will be different from now on. I will continue to walk every step but there, on the mountain, after that breathtakingly lovely walk and a whole day of Memorable Moments I feel I have penetrated a ring-pass-not.

18th June to Triacastela

Fab night's sleep in the iceberg. Today I will walk to Triacastela, a walk, according to my Michelin Guide, deserving of a red walker sign for a difficulty with a descent of 660 metres and steep. I will take care and put fleece in the toes of my socks to cushion my toes against hitting the crown of my boots on the descent. Paulo Coelho took a taxi from O Cebreiro to Santiago de Compostela, a whole 150 kilometres. He obviously didn't collect a Compostela. In fact I'm not even sure Shirley MacLaine did, she doesn't mention it either. I'll give it mention for sure, I will have earned it.

All pilgrims walk in silence as the hills and wind and forests seem to demand. The fleece in my boots cushions my toes; foxgloves and bluebells, significant of these cooler heights, line the banks. Alto de San Roque has a marvellous windblown pilgrim statue, many times life-size, on the crest of the climb; as his hand clutches his hat the wind is frozen forever in bronze. Coming into Hospital de la Condesa a young Italian passes me, stops: *I take a photo of you* he says and I ask: *why?* He indicates with his hands my polka dot ribbons, the rose in my scarf, my billowing skirt, the beribboned walking cane: *so spirituelle*, he smiles. I giggle. Only 144 kilometres to Santiago.

A slow-worm too slow to escape some deliberately cruel boot lies bleeding and only half crushed in the centre of the path, the centre where no one walks. I am saddened by such gratuitous mutilation for an accidental step on the creature would not have that affect. Would it make it less bewildering if I thought whoever left it to die so slowly mistook it for a snake? No. Nothing deserves such cruelty. It is a protected species in England but I am helpless to protect this one. I can witness, that's all.

Mount Poio at 1340 metres nearly does for me on the last sheer rocky and shale-slippery moment. Another young Italian reaches for my hand and steadies me, helps me on up. I don't stop at the café, too many pilgrims, but walk on past Fonfria and Biduedo to Filoval. Huge rock crystals are everywhere, some even placed as park benches. I stop at a new *albergue* and café in the last magical hamlet. Had I foreseen Drearcastila would be just that, drear, I would have set my *mochila* down in Filoval for the night. The food is so good, so plentiful and so tasty: gazpacho, the freshest bread and an *arroz con leche*. All made in the kitchen and eaten outside on a hilltop garden levelled out of the steep incline with spectacular views down to the valley and Triacastila.

Drearcastila – I walk the whole of the small town in search of an improvement on the dorm in *albergue* del Oribio with its washing lines on the busy street and chairs on the busy street but other pilgrims had walked faster than I and all rooms and dorms had been snaffled. I return with foreboding to my top bunk by the window of a dorm of sixteen and lay out my sleeping bag, have a hot shower, dress in the same skirt and check out the church.

23

A 007 Moment, Saintly Temptation and Camilla of the Three Swallows

One shower, one loo, in a mixed dorm of twenty-one. Not an inspiring experience at *albergue* del Oribio. Made worse by the snorer of all snorers in the bunk below me. His mate apologises as the snorer snores on, having a wondrous night's sleep while the rest of us suffered; *allergy,* he said, explaining his friend. Allergy, my eye! Keeping twenty people awake on a walk as gruelling as this is not an allergy, it's the height of selfishness. I lay sleepless. I prayed his mother in heaven would demand his company; I prayed he would stop breathing; I prayed he would fall out of bed; I prayed *wildly* for anything to happen to the poor unsuspecting, blissfully sleeping, bastard! And I tell you all, do not attempt to walk the Camino without bringing with you, tucked surreptitiously into your passport, a Licence to Kill.

The morning walk was magical. Of the two roads I chose the longer and the lower road to Samos where I sat in Lola's Café in the misty sunlight, eating and drinking all manner of deliciousness's while waiting for the tour of the extraordinary Benedictine monastery. The two young women who own the café proudly display their own *Compostelas* framed on the wall for all to see. Being there lifts my tiredness, the walk, cool and shady, is restorative. I don't know how I can walk without sleep, but I do.

The monastery is worth seeing, for all that so much was destroyed in a fire not so long back. Some rare manuscripts survived, and some of the contemporary frescos lining the walls of the cloisters, telling of the life of St Benedict and his raven, one of St Scholastica, his twin sister, are attractive. Benedict had refused her request that he wait awhile with her one evening as she sensed she was about to die. She invoked a storm so fierce that he could not leave to return to his hermitage. Great gal, never mess with a wild woman is the moral of that story. I would like Scholastica. I once sat in a bus going down to Dharamsala from a hill post further up the mountain with a Nyingmapa rainmaker. He was an impressive character too, and I wouldn't have dared cross him with thigh bones as hairpins in his mane and malas of miniskulls round his neck. Mermaids are another surprise in the monastery – painted on manuscripts, carved on the huge courtyard fountain.

I spend a couple of hours in Samos, the village itself only exists because of the monastery, but the day is pleasant and it takes a while before I decide to gird up my loins and get going on to Sarria.

Sarria is the beginning of the end. From here it is only 110 kilometres to Santiago. I learn that from here thousands of people begin their Camino, it is the last point from which one can start and still receive a *Compostela*. It will become a bed rush, so I'm told, but I don't quicken my pace or feel unduly worried, there will always be a bed. And there is – in Los Blasones, probably not the best choice of *albergue* in spite of being welcomed by Rufus Sewell without the glint in his eye. I beg a small room, of women only. I shouldn't have bothered. I was given a room with two bunks and in due time three other women arrived. One said her friend *snores only a leetle*. I shower, go off to eat and to explore.

I walk the mediaeval alleyways to find good food and many *albergues* that feel inviting. In the window of one is an 11th century Madonna that stops me in my tracks. She has all manner of tacky advertising labels on her. I am drawn in to rescue her. I swear she calls me. Alas, the *hospitalero* doesn't move from his seat and my plan to spirit her away in response to her being ignominiously ticketed is thwarted. I ask him if I can photograph her instead.

She is worth doing time for. She'll sit in my memory along with Borovinsky's exquisitely embroidered silk dressing gown I once stood in awe of in the Kars Museum when I was tripping across the Old Silk Road and about to descend on Marco Polo's bridge. As I stood there I gave full reign to the possibility of a year or three in a salt mine in Siberia but decided my suitcase of summer clothes would prove cold comfort against 60 degrees below freezing. A bit like St Claire's robe, these ancient things sing, *mine, mine,* as I re-encounter them this lifetime. It's a puzzle.

To sleep – or not to sleep. I didn't. The *leetle* snorer is oblivious even when I tweak her toe. She turns over and carries on snoring. The Licence to Kill would come in handy but I plump for something more calming. I lay turning the Rosary ring on my index finger; Tina gave me her own gold Rosary ring, taken spontaneously from her finger, after my pilgrim Mass and blessing at St Mary's a couple of days before I left for my Camino. After a few Hail Mary's I slip into the dual consciousness that meditation brings. The snoring is just as discomforting, sleep doesn't follow, but I dolphin-dose the night away, half awake, half asleep, as dolphins do to stop them sinking, drowning.

The young French Canadian girl above me doesn't sleep either. She is only nineteen, tall and Junoesque, with a mane of golden hair framing a very pretty face. She has walked from St Jean Pied de Port. We leave at 5.30 am. It is still dark. A Frenchman shines his torch for me when I fail to see the arrows, continues to turn and shine his light on puddles or at bends as I walk quite a ways behind, slowed by tiredness. The temperature is so humid my glasses fog up completely and keep sliding off my nose. Slowly daylight dawns and the Frenchman continues on apace.

The municipal *albergue* on the farther outskirts of Barbadelo looks marvellous; a plump and contented ginger cat sits on its porch. Fabulous walk again today, very rural, cobalt columbines cheer the wild verges, a granite walkway leads by a stream, springs and brooks really babble.

At Las Tres Golondrinos a welcome *donativo* table of delights provided by Camilla from Italy is set outside a huge barn. She has spread it with a gay table cloth and with all one could wish for breakfast. She has had a pretty *sello* made, of three swallows, *tres golondrinos*, which we stamp into our *credencials*. The Japanese woman who rescued me from under the barrier that led to nowhere by pushing my *mochila* flat against my back as I crawled under, while an unchivalrous Spaniard ignored my plight, is here. She throws her arms around me and we hug hugely, she tells me her name and I try to pronounce it. She is so brave; she speaks no English and no Spanish and is walking the whole way covered from head to toe so not a sunbeam can touch her pale skin. She is possibly forty, or sixty, plump, has a very sweet smile.

Copses of holm oak, banks of foxgloves, tiny hamlets with quaint names, Morgade, Mercadio. Morgade, five kilometres beyond Peruscalla where Camilla lives, has a charming restored *albergue*, an equally charming owner, and I am served tea and cake with a certain *panache*. Patricia is here, the pretty French Canadian. She tells me that for her the Camino changed after O Cebreiro. I nod, silently agreeing, but will not speak of why. What would words convey anyway, we share something ineffable.

I walk on. A man, an old rustic, comes towards me. He indicates that he wants to give me something, places a walnut in my hand. He asks if I will give it to Santiago and pray for him, he is too old, and not a little infirm, to go there himself. For good measure he hands one to a Frenchman who passes at that moment, the Frenchman looks at me and says, *we must do this, it is a trust.* I have no thought of not doing it, whether I am the first or the squillionth pilgrim who has been entrusted with a walnut and a prayer; it is indeed a trust, a holy pact. Such things often happened to me on the dusty paths of India decades ago, things like roses in answer to a prayer would just appear in the hands of a wandering sadhu who, in that instance, smiled, dropped them into my palm and walked on. A long walk such as this brings up old memories.

I think as I walk that the Camino can be walked in three ways: as a prescription (my plane leaves on xxx date and I must walk xxx kilometres every day to get to the end as prescribed by time); as a performance (I did the first one in 30 days, I can do better than that, race for 29, 28 ...); as a prayer (no plane booked, no time set, as long as it takes, always in awe). That's it, Three P's for a Pilgrim!

24

A Camino Miracle on Castromaior

Twenty kilometres today. A grand walk with only a few small hills brings me to Vilcachá and I decide to stop right here. No one is at home, so I sit in the sunny garden after washing out a couple of things, socks get so dusty, and hang them on the lines in a large open air barn which is near the entrance. A pair of dreadfully sick cats are lying on the grass on the opposite side of the garden. I have never seen such ill looking creatures, so weak and glazed eyed they might be dying. They are too weak to hunt or forage. I do not want to disturb them by going over to them; they haven't even registered my arrival. I wonder if I should stay here – such unhappy creatures are a sure indicator of the inner health of people too. Cats have a thin time of it in northern Spain as far as I can see, but these are beyond despair. St Francis didn't come this way that's for sure.

Eventually the owners of the *albergue* return. They are unfazed by the Feline Death Row on their lawn. I ask what is wrong with the cats, prepared to take my wet washing and continue walking. *They don't belong to us*, I'm told, *but the Australian next door hates cats and we think she might be poisoning them. We let them lie here in the sun, but we can't help them.* I have my *credencial* stamped, am shown into a lovely dormitory, choose a bunk, lay out my sleeping bag and then go next door. On the table in the courtyard there is an ugly notice signed by Suzanne warning people not to feed the cats, *they multiply*. Not *that* sick they don't, I fume, and knock, rather tentatively I must admit, heaven knows what kind of monster might appear, at Suzanne's door. There is no reply, and what will I say anyway? As I turn back to the street I hear horses hooves and look left to see three stunningly handsome Andalucians, almost plumed, one ridden by a highly costumed rider. They are riding to Santiago, and a marvellous sight they are. Two greys lead and a chestnut ridden by a woman follow a minute or so later.

During a chat with Gordon I'm told that Suzanne has no visa to stay in Spain and no licence to run her little illicit shop either. There is a veil of ill feeling, fiscal as well as feline, between the legitimate *albergue* and the illegitimate enterprise of their unattractive neighbour from Downunder.

I sigh, send the starving and sickly beings all the warmth and love I can without invading their space which would make them use up what energy they have in their effort to move away from a human. I wonder how they eat, but know it is too late now. They cannot hunt, and probably, hideously, are only able to crawl over to eat Suzanne's poison bait.

Later, a good and generous meal cooked by the two women and Anne Marie tells me if there is a snorer I can come down to the salon and sleep on the huge sofa. There is – and I do. It is a marvellous old building and I am content lying there listening to the wind and the rain on the window.

Breakfast was reasonable, Vilachá has no bar anyway. Gordon, who owns the place, has a marvellous story to tell of how he walked the Camino because he lost his memory after six small strokes, and is the subject, loosely, of Thea Hughes' novel of the Camino. He advises us not to go up the thousand steps to Portomarín, the rebuilt drowned village that lies beneath the central bridge we will walk over, or to be lead astray by the kilometre and a half detour around the new town only to come back down to turn left at a 200 metres from the same

145

steps, but to bypass it all, continue on past the steps, and walk back over the river by way of an old bridge further along to climb the hills to Hospital de la Cruz.

And that's what we all do, with great gratitude. It is a silvery morning, crisp and cool and misty, the weak sunlight glancing off the ghostly river under which lie the lives and memories of millennium. Gordon tells us the scheme set to gain from the drowning of the village only profited the planners and the engineers. He is a wry and cynical character and I suspect his insight is accurate.

Dripping in the humidity I reach the heights of Monte Torros, thankful for the slight plateau to Gonzar, and then lurch and stagger up the sheer vertical to Castromaior. It's only 11 kilometres from Vilachá, but imagine your lounge wall as being 700 metres vertical and that's about the incline of the walk, give or take a degree. I reach the second heights of the climb, Castromaior. As I come out of the forest to confront the road I lean heavily on my stick, catch my breath in great gulps, and send up a futile prayer. It has to be futile; I do not know a single human in northern Spain. *Holy Mary*, I puff and wheeze and pray *sans* hope, *please send me a taxi, a lift, anything...*

Hey! Zoé! I hear it. I think I am hallucinating from exertion, hear it again, and see across the road a car pull up and an arm cheerily waving. It is, miraculously, John, the third of the three charming Americans, John who drives (and who rescues animals in his home state) because he is unable to walk distances. He has pulled up and I am truly incredulous. I leap the ditch between where I stand and the road, run across and voila! jump in the car. He switches off the air-conditioning as I am dripping in the humidity and it would chill me. Angel! I am walking as Zoé, my simpler nom-de-plume for Downunder, though my Compostelas' will be recorded as Nigelle de Visme, in Latin.

146

We were wondering how you were, he said, *we hadn't seen you for a couple of days and I decided to look out for you ... I wasn't quite sure it was you coming up over that rise...*

Even I, used to such things as homely miracles, have to confess this one beats them all; although, walking into a closed restaurant in Rome, a city of merely 6 million people, to find the only remaining diner was Sue, the American woman I so wanted to keep in touch with from our meeting in Assisi, was also pretty impressive. I hadn't even prayed for that as the odds were so stacked.

John drives on to Palas de Rei, twelve welcome kilometres. His hotel is full, and lovely it looks too, one storey log cabins set in greensward ringed with pine and chestnut trees and wide gardens. The receptionist offers to phone a new *albergue* in the town for me and John drives me down. It proves perfect. I am taken to a ten bunk room; later a Spanish couple come in and take up residence at the other end. No one else comes in.

I walk the town in five minutes, find The Forge, a café with good food, a pilgrim three course meal with wine for 9€; lentil soup, chicken in brandy with rice, coffee. Later I walk up the Camino steps to a small church dedicated to San Tirso for a *sello* and am surprised by two Madonnas. One stands on a spiral shell. A Brazilian *peregrina,* more communist than Catholic she confides, is suddenly overwhelmed, as I am, by this symbol of, she tells me, the Great Earth Mother Goddess. She speaks in capital letters, and I hear them. We sit in equal awe, and a bit teary. Soft music of all the Ave Maria's ever written is playing. A Korean woman light candles, sits back down with her husband, they remain in prayer. I watch other pilgrims clump past the altar to the sacristy to get their *sello* without so much as a by-your-leave or a nod of acknowledgement, far less a genuflection, and I send my churlish thought to the Madonna of the Spiral Shell. *How,* I

147

ask Her, *can you bear such rudeness? In your own home!* I hear her smile and her words: *I love them all anyway!* I wish I did, but accept her instant admonition with a grin and a giggle.

A quiet night. The Spanish couple at the other end of the long large dorm are perhaps mid forties, rustic, very quiet, no lights on or noise; she is suffering. They are Camino babes, only began in Sarria. I show her the leg stretches, but I think she hurt too much even as she attempts them to understand their benefit.

The Brazilian *peregrina* had told me there are only three days walking to reach Santiago. Oh no, I think, shocked, how sad, my wonderful Adventure *can't* be over. She walks with her husband, they also began in Sarria, and she is suffering. I think of my weeks of aching and pain pain pain but saying, *one just gets on with it,* would be poor consolation, so I nod sagely.

25

Monsoon in Arzúa

I slept, almost well. The Spanish couple left so quietly. I hear them go, I can hear cats walking on carpet, but the pair are so careful in their quiet movements, so conscious that the door has a *handle* when they close it. How many people ignore the handle, slam a door instead of practising silence, stealth, and other good shamanic training towards invisibility? It seems to me that no one wants to be invisible anymore; everyone wants to be Very Noticed these days, with far too much Ego in their Cosmos. The need for noise affects and disturbs others, but has that thought ever penetrated their little homespun brains? I was once thrilled to read: *noise is the emblem of anarchy, the very fingerprint of entropy.* Something to do with the 2nd Law of Thermodynamics if I recall correctly. Reading it gave me such a sense of, *I'm alright then, it's the rest of the world that's out of kilter.* A most restorative revelation even to *my* homespun little brain.

This morning I can just lie here, John is driving to Melide today and will drop me there. I accept the lift with gratitude and grace and I can breakfast slowly. I love how magic just – *happens.* Leisurely I listen to pilgrims tapping their sticks along the road below the window; enjoy the muffled sounds of morning chatter; know I have three hours in which to write up my journal, have a quiet breakfast, idle the hours. I am charmed to see two Frenchwomen massaging each other's feet as they prepare to put on their boots. I collect my towel from the washing line, I washed it last night. It is still wet, so I'll pin it to my *mochila* to dry as I walk. Its sunny yellow will

149

surely attract the sun, it has been grey and drizzly overnight. I hear the clatter of horses' hooves and leap to the window – the three glorious Andalucians are walking past.

John arrives just as he said he would, we have a coffee before leaving. I ask him if he would mind a tiny detour; I discovered that a village on the way is called Leboreiro, meaning Place of Many Hares. My imagination plays – how can I resist the possibility of having a *sello* of a hare leaping over a scallop shell? Alas, we find no office or *albergue* and thus no *sello* in Leboreiro and we miss Melide, there is a huge festival in the main street and detours took us, as strangers to the town layout, far beyond the town. John drops me at Panabispo where the milestone to Santiago shows double figures. I feel momentarily bereft standing there as John hugs me and wishes me *buen Camino;* I sense I will not see any of the three Americans again.

I stand a moment, watch *peregrinos* as they enter the wooded path ahead of me. I am tired and wonder if knowing that I am nearing the end of my marvellous pilgrimage has thrown a cold douche of reality over me, dampened my wonder at walking an impossible dream? I shake off the feeling, photograph the milestone of Panabispo with its double red figures and walk on to Boente, climb another hill to Castañeda and make a steep descent into Arzúa.

A huge festival fills the streets, my intention to reach an *albergue* in the old part of town is hampered by crowds and I feel momentarily confused. I walk into a small hotel, they are full but recommend Hotel Begoña in easy reach down a side street. It isn't quite that easy, or quite so close, and I could have negotiated my way to the *albergue* as easily. But I am here, the room is blissfully quiet, the shower blissfully hot, I wash Everything and rig up my trusty washing line between balconied, but not accessibly balconied, windows and lay

150

down with my legs up, clean feet against the wall, recovering once more. That washing line, an invention with now well-rusted rings at each end, has travelled a few hundred thousand miles with me around the globe; I am fond of it, appreciate its humble purpose. It is lime green, a plaited cord of nylon and a length always perfect for the myriad spaces in which it finds itself strung anywhere over the world. That it is so amenable to infinite variety is a small and practical miracle in itself. I've grown so attached to its helpful adaptability and good temper even in the most trying surroundings that I hesitate to use it in open shared spaces these days – I might forget it, or it may prove unfaithful and take off with someone else...

My feet remind me they are cold stuck up there on the wall so I swing about and tuck them under the blankets, doze off for an hour or so before dressing and food foraging. The markets are closing down now, I have a not so good *pulpo,* dare I write that those I ate in neighbouring Castilla y León were vastly superior?

I return to my room just as a colossal clap of thunder rents the air and lightning bolts pierce the horizon in pirouettes. The heavens open. I have no need to go outside again and decide to send my *mochila* on to O Pedrouzo in dry comfort tomorrow so go down to arrange it with the receptionist. She takes my details and €3 for David who is the *mochila* taxi here and, as a by the way, tells me that there is to be live and very loud music in the town square tonight until 3 am. My heart sinks, the town square is just around the corner from my bedroom window. Furthermore I notice when I strung out my trusty washing line that the building opposite is a dosshouse for old hobos a few of whom were already reeling below the window. Noise! But now, the monsoon. I love rain. Love monsoons. And the storm of all storms, liquid carnage, washes out play, the bandstand is flooded, the music called off and the old soaks in the hostel opposite my bedroom are silenced too. I watch from my windows as the rain gathers in

151

rivers to flood down the street. It is dramatic and I have a wonderful night's sleep.

The sky is clear when I wake, the air filled with ions so negative after the storm they positively dance in front of me as I step out. Today's walk to O Pedrouza is only nineteen kilometres. I take the wrong turn, again. But a sixth sense alerts me and I turn back and round a corner to see a trail of *peregrinos* heading down a narrow alleyway left. It is a lovely easy walk, my heart and back are light, the sun shines through clouds which have been cleansed of their rain burden. I am charmed by the *hórreos*, especially the ones with protective symbols. What better way to protect the grain that will give you life than to hedge ones' bets by using Catholic as well as pagan symbols on the roof apexes of these grain stores, life stores.

Another *donativo* table appears and I choose a banana, but to my dismay have no coins. Nor have the German couple who pause and take. I take, but feel so ill at ease I write an IOU to Felix for my banana. I sign it, promise to pay next time. I don't know that I will do the Camino ever again but if I do I will honour the 50 cents. Perhaps someone reading my IOU will indulge in an act of random kindness and leave Felix what I owe.

I recall Caroline's Camino with rain rain rain from when she entered Galicia; I remember Gerald Kelly's misery as he recounted wet, wet, wet right through Galicia; and I thank my lucky stars that the rain has passed – and I am in Galicia. I reach the grave of a woman; it has a photograph, she is younger than I and died while doing her second Camino. While I digest all that is written, breathing in a marvellous smell of eucalyptus oil as I stand at the edge of the eucalyptus forest which will take me all the way to Santiago, another couple pause next to me, one reads out loud to the other.

They are Australian and my Alice in Wonderland moment is poised to resurface.

26

O Pedrouzo, O Mochila, O, O'Reilly Street!

Eucalypts on the Camino and Two Australians add to my Alice in Wonderland moment. The Australians are my own vintage give or take a year or two and I ask where they are from – and refrain from rolling my eyes heavenward at *Australia*. I think to myself *well naturally you're from Australia, your accent is a geographical chant,* but ask civilly – *but where in Australia?* Americans always do likewise, as if we, the rest of the English speaking world didn't know by the sound of their voice where they come from! When I'm asked I always reply *Glastonbury* – and to a good ear the next question arises: *but you have a slight, er, um,* as they hesitate – *ah yes,* I say, *you are right, a slight Australian twang about my vowels...* Cutting to the chase is my *modus operandi,* I want to get to the main point with as little flimflam as possible. It's one of my many irritating traits, I know!

Their answer floors me: *Townsville.* I drop my momentary prickles, *Townsville!* Floods of memories rise up. I lived there for years, went back last August to stay with the dearest of friends, ached leaving it, and them, again. Townsville, where I lived as a child and rescued Blueboots the legendary Strand lifer whose not too kind owner walked him up and down the old Strand for years, giving children pony rides on a back scarred and raw with sores from a badly fitting saddle. I saved and begged and scrounged and rescued the twenty-two year old Blueboots for a tenner. Loved him passionately, dreamed, hopelessly, the poor tired creature into my Prince Hal – Pat Smythe was every horsey girls heroine at the time. When we

154

moved south my mother refused to let me bring Blueboots, sold him back to his abuser on my last day away at school. I never forgave her for betraying the poor soul. Thirty-five years later the Fates brought me back to Townsville to James Cook University to write my thesis, and I fell in love with the Tropics all over again. I loved the clouds! Full of dark promise, heavy, and rich; dark promise like the dark mystery of the subject of my thesis of discovery: discovery of the Black Madonna. The name Townsville brings to my mind's eye a circular memory, a sense of completion, an etheric Camino pathway as it were, right here in a *eucalyptus* forest.

Oh, I say in surprise and delight, *it's my most favourite city; I used to live in Mundingburra!* Their response stops me right there in the eucalypt forest: *we used to live in Mundingburra.* We exchange names and I, who am thrilled at the coincidence, tell Sue I lived in O'Reilly Street and she responds with: *we lived in O'Reilly Street too.* My Alice in Wonderland Moment assumes the Cheshire Cat's Grin.

They lived at number 26, I lived at 33 on the opposite side of the road. *When?* we ask simultaneously, and discover we lived in O'Reilly Street Mundingburra during the same years, and through the horror of the 1998 cyclone. Their side of the street suffered terribly, the park behind them flooded and all the even numbers of all the houses went under water. 33 O'Reilly was high set, on seven foot stumps, and the street on the odd-numbered side was higher too, the flood waters only reached my carport, came up to my waist. The cyclone coincided with a King Tide, Townsville was cut off, declared a National Disaster Zone, cars were washed away, people drowned, outside communication was severed, residents were told to remain indoors for days – though on the fourth day a friend and I managed to get to the Strand to leave food for the stray cats. The old Strand itself was destroyed. Driving through the streets then was like driving through a war zone. The weir at the end of O'Reilly Street was flooded, the swollen Ross River a constant, terrifying, booming roar I could hear from my bedroom for weeks as it thundered over the weir.

Townsville population runs around 170,000 over forty odd suburbs. I lived in one of those suburbs and count close friends on less than the fingers of one hand. The odds are low, but do Sue and Tony happen to know them? They certainly do, attended the funeral of a mutual friend only weeks before, now live in a marvellous skyline apartment complex and neighbour to another mutual friend, have links with the House of Prayer, the best little sanctuary in Oz and the affinities, for me, simply grow curiouser and curiouser. But couples are couples, and my excitement is singular and solely significant to me. As aware as I am of this I still allow my affection for that past time and loved place to interrupt their walk.

We reach O Pedrouzo and the yellow arrow, rather shabbily painted, points right to a bar and to the continuation of the path through the forest. The next milestones show a kilometre marking that doesn't accord with my reckoning of the distance to O Pedrouzo. Tony looks at his map, O Pedrouzo is *back there*. They are headed for Amenal where they have pre-booked a hotel; about now we are standing in the forest at San Antón. Oh. A Korean girl walks briskly towards us, she overshot O Pedrouzo too, misled by the false yellow arrow. She and I trudge back together, the yellow arrow was painted by the barman, leading us to the last bar in town, his. The town itself is *left*, and left by a long chalk and a long walk. She is kind, the young Korean girl, concerned that my venerable self will find the municipal *albergue*, walks with me through the town to where I sent my *mochila* and, *buen Camino*, we wish each other as she leaves me to find her own privately run *albergue* where her friends are meeting.

156

To my dismay my *mochila* is not here. The brusque *hospitalera* tells me they refuse to receive *mochilas*, their reason is lost on me and I begin to fret. I am told to go back to a café where my *mochila* might have been dropped off. It wasn't. I sit down, quite stunned. What on earth can I do? I feel like weeping and three kind Italian men make every fuss of me and phone everywhere and then walk with me to the private *albergue* of Porte de Santiago and voila! the kind *hospitalero* there had accepted my errant *mochila*. The men chuckle when they see my red and white polka dot ribbons, and more, that my *mochila* is a Ferrino. One of them has a Ferrino: *the best,* he smiles.

The *hospitalero* asks if I am staying, and out of my mouth pops, *thank you so much for all your help, but no, I think I want to go on to Amenal, and I think I'd like a taxi.*

I stand at a loss as I say this, why not rest here? As the words form and fall into being the snorer who only *snores a leetle* is signing in with her daughter. I suspect my answer is a response from somewhere very deep inside me, from a place of body wisdom that knows more than I do how exhausted I am after thirty-nine days on the road. The thought of a hotel in Amenal, where Sue and Tony have pre-booked, beckons. A real night's sleep... I only have tomorrow to walk – into Santiago. The *hospitalero* runs to the street to call me a taxi, I reach over the desk to stamp his official *sello* in my *credencial,* I want to remember this place, his kindness; the Italians are sitting in the lounge, surprised I am leaving. The taxi driver is young-ish (anyone round here is young compared to me) and speaks enough English. We reach Amenal, it's only 2 kilometres along the road, but there are no rooms. I dread going back to the *albergue* and a dorm for my final night on the Camino. My taxi *gallant* takes my life in his hands – *I make phone call for you* he says and I don't care where it is he is offering to drive me, it will be perfect.

And so I come to Lavacolla. Once upon a time there was a pool here at Lavacolla where all pilgrims ritually washed the dust off their heels as well as their clothes, and symbolically their soul, to prepare for the great walk tomorrow. I pause, amazed at how appropriate, how symbolic a place, I have been brought to for my own last night. My taxi driver has a hint of the angel about him, this is his choice for me, an hotel close to the airport and opposite the small laneway that will lead me on to the Camino tomorrow. I am offered a perfect room, at *peregrina precios*, and find my window faces that very laneway. I tip my taxi driver and thank him just as the storm of all storms bursts overhead. The whole of Nature is washing me in preparation! Waving goodbye I race back inside, shower and make myself ready to go down to eat what will be the best meal I've had in Galicia: organic *cidre*, langoustines, *filet mignon*, steamed vegetables, homemade crème caramel and a bottle of local mineral water, all for €15, a real extravagance and a gift from my Secret Agent.

The torrential rain over Lavacolla, the washing place, is a fitting baptism for my walk into Santiago tomorrow. I wash the ribbons on my boots, on my backpack, on my walking stick and on my hat in preparation. After walking 700 kilometres my dear uncomplaining feet have a little moan on each little toe. Fleece for them tomorrow. Tomorrow, too, I can crack open my tiny phial of hairspray, my lippy, the red and white polka dot Alice band bought in Burgos. I spend a couple of hours writing up my journal; so many complexities woven into a day. I note down that passing through St Eulalia a sung "welcome" greets me, an old pilgrim song, as I walked past a box with a speaker wired up on a fence. I'd stood in front of the contraption and burst out laughing at its ingenuity.

Tonight I feel my epic pilgrimage has expiated every sin possible to commit in one lifetime and, having resisted the desire to murder a snorer or six, am glowingly confident I will have earned my right to wear a scallop shell in whatever form of jewellery I find when I reach Santiago! The storm has blown past, the sunset, as I look from my window, glows over Santiago, is a glory. I am blessed, cosy, safe and dry and I settle down to sleep the sleep of the just.

27

Santiago and a Strange Angel

I wake, it's still dark, I slept superbly well, sleep was deep and I am excited. I paddle down to the darkened foyer, surprise a dozing night watchman, check the time, 05.40, perfect. Breakfast, at 6 o'clock is a too modest affair, the baker hasn't yet arrived. However the coffee is good and I am eager to walk. Pilgrims of long ago would wash themselves, "lava", before setting off for the final walk of 15 kilometres from Lavacolla to Santiago. The storm was my cleansing, my ribbons washed in preparation. I return to the room, use the very last of my *fusskraft menta* on my knees, swaddle both little toes in fleece, clean my teeth, NOK and 1000mile sock my feet – anoint and swaddle – put on my boots with their clean and gay ribbons, swing my *mochila* into place and step out into very fresh air. I breathe in a prayer. The skies are leaden, the storm has left a tired drizzle in its wake, I cross the quiet highway, walk down the narrow lane, turn left at its end and I'm on my way. Dawn is beginning to break.

I come to the eucalyptus forests. A Spanish Benedictine, Father Salvado, brought them here from Western Australia where he had founded New Norcia, the first Benedictine Abbey in Australia, in 1846. His transplants took root, multiplying with more alacrity than his converts to Christianity Downunder. There are hundreds of thousands of eucalyptus in Galicia, I doubt it's a good thing, ecologically speaking, but the accompanying fragrance of eucalyptus oil is wonderful, invigorating, stimulating. In the open fields lie Galician blond cows, pretty faced, somnolent as the light drizzle coats them.

Some of the Way is true to the last 40 days, cool, shady, lots to observe, hills and dales. On and on I walk pass sleeping villages to: Monte do Gozo! This marks the end really. I walk a long ways left, cross fields, to the *albergue* for a *sello* and even further off the Way to climb the mount itself to photograph the splendid statues of two pilgrims pointing in joy as they see for the first time the spires of the great Cathedral of Santiago. It is a thrilling and lonely moment, no one else has taken the detour to see them. It is drizzling and dark, the mist is thick, but just as I puff my way up the hill the sun momentarily lightens the mist for a moment to light their backs. No worthy photos, but I attempt a couple. The statues are huge, easy for them to see the spires of Santiago – at five foot tall I barely reach the hem of their shoulder capes, wouldn't have seen much even on a clear day. Elation is part of the amalgam of feelings I am filled with right now.

The walk into Santiago seems long. I buy a croissant from a surly baker, a woman, who obviously doesn't want to be open at this early hour – for it is early, and wet, and I may be the only customer for a while. The suburbs go on and on, busy intersections confuse me, pilgrims walk past me fast and purpose-bent. At a place of five directions I ask the way of a pilgrim coming towards me, he is a strangely babbling German and refuses to simply point to the right choice of five ways but launches into each and every way that each and every way could get me to my destination. Frustrated, I say, *stop! I am very tired, please just point me the quickest way* and at that moment another walker comes alongside and says quietly, *follow me.*

He proves a strange angel, a loner, an American who has been here many days, comes here many times, calls me *ma'am* and is so excessively polite I almost doubt his sincerity. It makes me uncomfortable. Perhaps I am tired. He walks me all the way to the Cathedral and I see on my right the Seminario Maior. A bell of remembrance, Maeve in Glastonbury told me to stay

161

here. I excuse myself from my companion and go inside to register and book a room. It takes a while, their special pilgrim rooms are fully booked, I take a room at the hotel price for one night, ask directions for the Pilgrim Centre so I can get my well-earned *Compostela*. Outside the strange angel is sitting on the wall in the drizzle, I am chastened at his patience, we walk to the pilgrim centre, my delay has lengthened the queue of arrivals. My strange angel tells me to sit on the wall inside the compound, he will stand in the long queue for me. He has, however, as we walk down through the arcade and the steps, made strange allusions that reveal an odd way of thinking, my antennae prickles through my tiredness. I am grateful and cautious. Yet all went well, after an hour he reaches the hallowed door and we swap places.

This is the *summum bonum* of my pilgrimage, this one minute moment while a charming young man writes my name in Latin on a fancy certificate, a new design, with Saint James in full colour, yet truly my feelings do not accord with the gravitas of the moment. It is too hurried, and when all said and done, the *Compostela* only a piece of paper. I walked the Camino, I have three *credencials* to remind me forever, I earned them, they have been with me all the way, how I received my first one, blessed by Holy Mary of Glastonbury and Saint Teresa of Avila, little short of a miracle. I do not share the obvious thrill that some pilgrims are sharing, shouting as they wave the rolled certificates in their tubes patterned with scallop shells. Once again I am out of kilter.

The strange angel walks me to the monastery of St Francis, but we find it has just closed for the morning and will re-open at five in the evening. I will return for my St Francis *Compostela* then, this one will carry meaning for me. I am so tired, I need a coffee, and actually, I need something to eat. My strange angel insists on my following him, he is fast-paced, quite far ahead but keeps looking round to see if I am following. Suddenly my brain goes on walkabout and my feet slew sideways into a café. He is too far ahead and doesn't hear my call. I must surely buy him a coffee for his kindness. I sink into a chair, alas there is nothing to eat but sweet things and I need a serious protein hit before I collapse, but I settle for a coffee to settle my brain. As I sit there the strange angel walks past on his return, I wave, he is too fast, doesn't notice me in the café, looks intent. I sink back down, relieved, actually. So thank you, Marvin of New Mexico, you were an angel of the moment.

I make my way back to the Seminario, focus on showering, changing, eating. As I pass the restaurant in the cloisters, with its grand name *Comedor Monumental*, who walks out but: Jüergen! Jüergen of the roses and the rosemary! Jüergen my best bunk buddy of so many weeks ago! We stand speechless, then hug hugely, delight tangible. He has been here for a week and more, helping arriving pilgrims find their way. Photographs! Emails! "When I first saw your pilgrim skirt and the bows on your boots I knew I wanted to know you", he tells me, laughing. We haven't seen each other for ages, not, since Agés, many weeks ago.

It is still only the morning on the first day of my arrival in Santiago. What more surprises can be in store. The pleasure of seeing Jüergen releases a euphoria that queuing for my *Compostela* had failed to do, I can acknowledge the wonder of the whole walk, feel a rising sense of anticipation at just being *here*, in Santiago de Compostela. I have been on my pilgrimage for forty days and forty nights, a biblical reckoning, and Jüergen tells me it is the Feast Day of Saint John the Baptist, the Botafumeiro will be swung at midday, a Pilgrim Mass offered to bless us all – and I must hurry to find a space amongst the thousands.

163

28

"That Rare Thing, an English Catholic!"

24th June 2014: San Martin de Pinario really is an actual seminary and very grand. I smile to myself, nuns don't have anything like the same start in life! I lunch at the Comedor Monumental, busy waiters, grand names for the menu selection, mediocre truth on the plates when they arrive. But the dining room is true to its name – monumental. A vast vaulted stone block ceiling makes it another cloister in appearance, a marvellous room. Just after showering and donning my clean Macabi skirt and other top I did pop across to the Cathedral at midday, but the dense crowds overwhelm me and claustrophobia sends me scuttling back to San Martin de Pinario. I rue my failure to see the famous Botafumeiro, the world's largest thurible that takes up to a dozen men to control the swing of its vast arc from end to end of the transept; know it is only used on Feast Days and Holy Days now, but shrug off the once only opportunity with the consolation that I have had miracles all along the way – I am full.

I return later to the Cathedral, empty now but for the delicious swirls of incense still thickly veiling the altar, and look for the English chapel with its copy of Our Lady of Walsingham sitting on her Throne of Wisdom. A copy of course, from another copy, as she was, with Our Lady of Glastonbury and every other Lady, burned on the pyres of Smithfield at the Reformation. She's a pretty statue, and very 'English', with none of the quirky authenticity of expression that marks her mediaeval sisters whom I've met on my pilgrimage. I slide my prayer for England, once known throughout the world as Our Lady's Dowry, a dedication of her uncle Joseph of Arimathea, under the grill; it continues its slide along the polished floor to stop underneath the statue. I remain a few moments, then look for the crypt and the reliquary of Santiago; here I say a prayer and roll the walnut right along the floor. Done. I don't walk up the ancient staircase to thank Santiago in his silver casing, yet. Something stops me. This day is a moment by moment time capsule and I must remain obedient to its shifts and suggestions.

I go on to San Francisco, love the simplicity of the nave as I walk down to the sacristy to collect my St Francis *Compostela*. There are few of us. The attractive Brazilian couple in their pink clothes whom I met in Palas de Rei are here, he grins and says, *You are that rare thing, an English Catholic! I have not met one before, and you are a woman and you walk alone, from Pamplona!* He places his hand over his heart in wonder and we all burst out laughing. They began at Sarria, a mere eighty or so kilometres back.

My turn comes, I hand over my *credencials*. The old Franciscan friar sitting at the other end of the table smiles and blesses me in the name of St Francis while a woman writes my names and hands me my scroll. I try to tell the dear friar that it was because of St Francis when I was in Assisi that I walked the Camino in this, his 800th Anniversary Year. And I burst into tears. The Brazilian couple burst into tears. Everyone there gets teary! I go and sit on the front pew. The Brazilian couple join me, point out the amazing image of the triangle – the Holy Trinity – in the apex of the ceiling in which is an Eye, the Eye of God. I *am* amazed and amazement stops the teary moment just-like-that. The only other times I have seen this symbol is in Romania, in an Orthodox Church, and in Turkey, in an Islamic Mosque.

In the 1980's on my Old Silk Road jaunt I had rescued a kitten in a wild little town named Siirt in the Kurdish region of Turkey and had taken it into a café to give to the owner. He had a constant font of hot milk for making *salep* (from orchid root) which seemed to me just what a kitten needed. The kindly man, a Kurd and proud of it, accepted his new charge happily. Muslims have a great affection for cats; Mohammed refused to disturb his favourite asleep on his robe, called for a knife when it was time for prayers, cut around the garment so as not to wake puss. Love the story. Back to my kitten and the Eye of God – the café owner said I had seen this hapless mite through the Eye of Allah, Eye of God, and pointed to the mosque, urging me to go and see for myself. It is a rare symbol to be in a mosque, and would devolve into the ubiquitous blue glass eye. My man said he had nothing warm for the kitten to sleep on, tiles were cold, kitten was too tiny to climb onto a chair, he wouldn't be home until late, his home had no phone thus he couldn't call his wife to bring in something warm. The kitten's rescue began to assume the length of a shaggy dog story; except that all was true. I watched the man's gentleness as he held the tiny creature in the palm of his hand, placed it on the café counter to drink warm milk from a saucer. I scurried off to an antique carpet dealer, explained the plight. He produced the softest piece of antique kilim, looked at me quizzically for a moment, there had to be an exchange. I unfurled my hand in which was clutched what was left of my loose change, a pittance. He graciously accepted what I had, and told me I had seen the kitten's need through the Eye of Allah. I was quite drawn by the Eye of Allah – and here it is above me.

I am quite silent. We three sit for a long time, listening to the sublime polyphonic music St Francis would have known. *Now* I feel something.

As an anti-dote to all this emotion I wander back along the street shops to look for earrings. Retail therapy will ground me, the purchase of earrings will have a certain solemnity about it, will honour my epic pilgrimage. I giggle as I think it. Scallop shells in lime green enamel and silver draw my attention, but not quite enough. Silver and black enamel make me pause, but not long enough. I am drawn into a gay little trinket shop opposite the Seminary, playing zappy Galician folk songs and there! in the cabinet on the wall as I go in is ... a pair of poppy earrings! Poppy Peregrina! They are wondrous, wooden or something like that, painted red with the stamens needle-etched in black. They are so stunningly appropriate and so little price, I buy without a second's delay, put them on at once. They look marvellous. Poppy Peregrina has been confirmed! I hurry back to my room, stow my San Francisco *Compostela* safely with Santiago's and realise I am just in time for the evening prayers in English over in the Cathedral.

With such earrings I am complete, as it were, ready to bounce over to the Cathedral with a light heart, am only a minute late, squeeze past the squashed together chairs filled with pilgrims, find a seat at the front of the horseshoe layout, turn, sit down and hear a loud, *Zoé!* coming at me from two directions at once.

The meditative silence is shattered, thank heavens the prayers proper haven't quite begun, and I see Ann on my left and Ela, her face alight with delight, calling, *I'm so happy to see you!* from the half-circle of chairs opposite me. I am thrilled too, we modify our excitement, prayers begin, we pray happily, listen to a few Camino chronicles and share a fitting silence together, united in our achievement.

Outside Ela hugs me hugely, tells me I am the one person she most wanted to meet again, she asked all along the Camino but no one could say where I was. *You floated along*, she said, to my astonishment. Floated? I puffed and wheezed and staggered and perfected the pilgrim's lurch very early in the piece, no way could my perambulations be seen as floating! She insists it was how I looked. Ann has to leave, says we will meet tomorrow. Ela tells me Vanessa and John left for Finisterre yesterday and Christina should be back tomorrow. Ela was too tired to walk on, she took a day trip by bus to Finisterre and Muxia, recommended it for me. The other person she wanted to see again was Jüergen – *but he's here in Santiago* I say. Alas I cannot say where, I do not know. We will pray for just another miracle. She walks over to the seminary with me, she is also staying there, and takes a wondrous photo of me with my poppy earrings, my red and white polka dot Alice band – which she hadn't seen before, hoots of laughter at this – the ditto *mnemonics* on boots and backpack and stick.

I am very very tired and very happy; it is the most perfect end to my first day in Santiago.

So Endeth the First Day ...

29

Vive La France, Air Traffic is on Strike!

I wake too early and lay fretting that I must trail about Santiago looking for another room as I was given the only vacancy here, a hotel room at that, and that for one night only. But *something* urges me to go downstairs and ask the night staff ... who proves so much more accommodating than the crisp Miss of yesterday's day staff. He can give me a pilgrim room from tonight, for four nights, at the pilgrim price of €23 including breakfast. I'm so relieved. I can now find a flight, explore and sleep, sleep, sleep...

I ask him about flights to Paris, to retrace my flight path home to Bristol. *Ah*, he tells me, *but not to Paris, their Air Traffic is on strike again and all flights are suspended for the next seven days.*

Oh. Double Oh. He books my room for a further two days as a precaution. I'll sort out flights later today. I dread the return. I want the Camino Adventure to go on forever even though my body is saying *can't, can't!* and I have promised I won't make it suffer Ever Again.

Now I am securely accommodated for the rest of my stay I can relax. I will take over my Pilgrim's Cell in the attic at 10 o'clock. I repack, rest, and go down to breakfast at 7.30, first off the starting line. A Dutch woman asks to sit at my table; her story, and why she walked the whole Camino moves me, she is very teary and with good reason. She lost *forty* kilos in weight along the way. I sit open-mouthed, I had gained a few kilos myself, but I would not want the story she was telling me in order to hasten such a weight-loss. I cannot remember her story, didn't commit it to my journal and it has blown away on the wind; pilgrims have many stories and pilgrims hear many stories. We hug and wish each other love and happiness.

I drift over to the shop in the cloisters, which sells all manner of religious memorabilia and I ask a pointless question. All along the Camino are marvellous statues and references to *peregrinos*, but I want, along with the poppy and a scallop shell, an image of a *peregrina*. *Ah,* smiles the wise woman behind the counter, *but we have the real Peregrina not so far from Santiago; la Divina Peregrina.*

Instantly I am alert. I must visit Pontevedra, she tells me, on the *Camino Portugués.* Three and a half days walk south, and three and a half days back – or I can catch a train, the return journey will take two hours. I opt for the train, a no-brainer in my state. 140 kilometres round trip, I can barely believe how only days ago I happily walked such distances; 700 kilometres is already disappearing into the mists of memory. La Divina Peregrina will be my Adventure for tomorrow. I'm thrilled, I will be more rested by then, and open for anything.

10 o'clock and I move up to my attic. It is ideal, and so suited to a pilgrim. A tiny cell, a plain single bed with snowy sheets and a thick chocolate coloured wool blanket, a scallop shell on the iron bed-head, a tiny desk and chair, a capacious cupboard and a small cubicle with a shower, wash basin and loo. The high attic windows run the width of the room and the view of turrets and towers is marvellous. I am happy here.

Now I must book my flight. I feel unaccountably helpless, as if the effort of strategies needed to survive the last six weeks has drained me of quotidian functioning. I, who can organize a trip to Angkor Wat at the drop of a map, am inexplicably threatened by the mere thought of navigating cyber space for a flight home, now compromised by the airport strike in Paris, my route plan to Bristol. I actually send up a prayer for help.

In the street between the Seminary and the back of the Cathedral people are milling. I scan to see if anyone I know is there, yes! there is Ela, and beyond her range of vision, but I can see from the Seminary steps, is Jüergen! I run across and am hailed by Sister Aileen from the English prayer group, all my prayers answered at once. I tell Sister Aileen I will be back in two minutes, call Ela who turns, point out Jüergen, calling his name as I do. Another grand photo-shoot to mark the moment; Jüergen is about to catch the bus to the airport to fly home.

I return to Sister Aileen, tell her my dilemma. She has the perfect solution, Father John from Ireland is computer savvy and will help me after English Mass in the Cathedral but English Mass extends to coffee so we shift our appointment to after Pilgrim Mass at noon. And ... a nun with the voice of an angel is singing. It is a long Mass, the Pilgrim Mass, and I take the moment to climb the stairs behind the High Altar to thank Santiago. I am alone. Exactly as I reach the silver statue, Angel voice sings an Allelujia, her rich soprano pierces the transept. I feel an upwelling of tears and put both hands and my forehead to rest on Santiago's silver back. Tears flow unimpeded. I thank Santiago, Holy Mary and St Francis and Jeff and Olivia and Caroline and Tina and Thérèse and Everyone who has made my pilgrimage possible. And the tears continue. I'm not crying exactly, but the tears are coming from a place below words, before words were formed, and I suspect many and many a pilgrim has known their own tears here before me.

I return to Mass. It is a huge Cathedral and it would take a search party to find a lost soul. Comings and goings are all part of it and no one bats an eye at my absence or return as I perch on a stone plinth near the altar. I watch intently as men assemble, the huge silver thurible is being lowered. Lo and behold a grateful pilgrim has paid for the Botafumeiro to be swung and I have a front row view. The spectacle is awesome and I take a number of blurred photos. A holy moment, and so unexpected.

Then off to the cyber café with Father John. No planes going to Paris, no going via Dublin either, Aer Lingus flights one way are £300. I am getting stressier and stressier. I would sooner walk another 700 kilometres than tackle air fares, flights and cyber space right now. Father John finds me a flight to Gatwick from Santiago with easyJet for €103 and a National Express bus to Bristol. Practicalities over, I buy Father John lunch and introduce him to hot chocolate Spanish style.

Siesta then, in my pilgrim room. Up here in the attic I feel like Gertrude, Countess of Groan, but for the lack of a furlong of white cats trailing after me! I doze off and surface at four, dress in everything I have, the weather has turned cold even though it is high summer. I head off to buy my train ticket to Pontevedra and to book my trip to Finisterre when I see, coming up the steps of Plaza Obradoiro, Gene and Sandy, last met in León three weeks ago. They have walked the Camino prompted by Martin Sheen's The Way; began in Pamplona and have walked enough. They accompany me to book the trip to the End of the Known World, for Saturday. And so Endeth the Second Day ...

172

30

La Divina Peregrina

26th June 2014. Bliss to sleep alone and wake to the sound of the Cathedral bells. How magical this long adventure, how can I bear to go back to Chaingate Court? Truth is, I can't, so I must Ask and wait to Receive.

Sat with Cindy at breakfast. She was having a teary moment like I had yesterday with Wilhelmina and *her* teary moment. El Camino ... how can words touch the depths where only tears hold and tell our stories, our walk, our Camino?

Cindy began ten weeks ago in Le Puy: *Wonderful*, she says, *silent, solitary, beautiful; mountains and valleys and marvellous auberges, mochila transport, superb food and facilities – and you can travel with the transport for 15€ if you don't feel like walking that day.* Well, it is France isn't it, I muse as she tells her story, almost tempted to think myself another walk. Feet come into the story. Cindy tells me she developed tendinitis so severely and so painfully she could only walk on her heels, for *miles and miles*. At St Jean Pied de Port a man told her she *must* teach her feet to walk properly – and they didn't know how to. She had to go on Internet to research a way to re-teach her feet by using her brain to *tell* them the movements: heel first, roll the foot, lift from the ball and toes ... She cried as she told me, because no-one had understood, she couldn't tell anyone what she was going through.

I am awed at her perseverance, she has walked 777 kilometres from Le Puy to St Jean and still had 777 kilometres to go before she would sit here in Santiago and tell me her foot story. Me of all people, whose foot story and cellular memory is so similar. *Oh*, I say, *oh Cindy I know exactly what you mean*, and I share my wheelchair, cellular memory, teaching my feet to walk over grassy tussocks and ripples in the sand by thinking them through the movement until their own natural cellular memory is re-awoken. Cindy listens intently, her eyes flood with tears. She *knew*, and she knew because I *under-stood*, our sharing in perfect *accord*, what a metaphor – we *under-stood*. How can we, she, speak of these things to many? I feel a great warmth for Cindy, she had her sixtieth birthday along the Way; she looks about twelve.

As Cindy leaves Ela comes in and sits with me. She tells me the floating bit again and I burst out laughing. I admit others have said that too, and I find it quite incongruous. I don't doubt their truth or their eyesight and all I can think of is that Angels must have been carrying me! Angels, Holy Mary or Santiago because I did not have one blister as if my feet did not touch the ground! Inside me, I tell Ela, I plodded and lurched with tiredness as I walked slow step by slow step all the way. Ela promises to send me the photos she took, and especially the ones of Simone and I toasting socks over the fire when we all first met at the Paulo Coelho *refugio* with Jüergen.

Now I am at the train station with my ticket for Pontevedra, my train leaves at 11.11. It is cold today, 13 C and the end of June.

When I bought my poppy earrings the young saleswoman told me the witch, the wise woman, *la bruja*, is good luck throughout northern Spain and different *brujas* carry different attributes: good health, happiness, wealth, safe travel (well, they'd know about that flitting about on broomsticks), love, longevity and so on. How different from Puritan England where the very word is pejorative and has long since lost its wiser truth. I bought myself a tiny, less than the size of my thumb, *la bruja* made of clay while in Santo Domingo de la Calzada, I love her cheery grin and her blue hood, like my poncho, her cockle shell and her stick and gourd. I haven't seen such a wee happy one since then. This morning I unwrap her and stand her next to my water glass; I love her to pieces, such a funny and perfect image of me, the old cackling crone of the Camino!

11.11 and the train departs at the exact tick of the station clock. I settle by a window, sift and sort my morning stories, create mental space for my Encounter. I am sizzling with anticipation. A super train it is, fast and clean with clever seating that can swing according to direction of travel. I'm happy with forward, and the hour slips by quickly. Pontevedra! Oh, civilization and hundreds of people – I'm such a hedgerow planting, happiest with fields and dormice – but I find yellow arrows and a cockleshell to follow through the elegant streets of elegant shops to – Plaza Peregrina!

I am here, and there is the baroque church and it is open and I enter to stand transfixed at Nuestra Señora, la Divina Peregrina. She is wonderful! She is gorgeous! Just gorgeous, standing high above the altar She is dressed in a cape and long robe (is this familiar, oh indeed it is!) and wears a wondrous pilgrim hat, its wide brim turned back and decorated with a scallop shell, a long staff with a gourd for water in Her right hand and a little Jesus perched precariously in Her left hand. She is looking straight ahead, at you and me as we walk in the door, actually. And Her face, so quiet and proud, just like I feel after such a Long Walk. This is my homecoming, this is my acknowledgement, She and I, we've done it! Not for nothing do we share birthdays! The 8th of September, *such* a good day to have been born unmothered into the world and to eventually discover the Mother of All had me in Her sights all along! This is the *real* full circle of my pilgrim path on earth. She smiles. I smile back. My very insignificant camera works a miracle in the dim light and the great distance between us: *Take one photo* I ask of it, *perfectly. Thank You,* I smile again. I swear She says, *you see, I've been with you always, all through your pilgrimages, all through your loneliness, all through your losses, how did you survive so much? Because I was there with you, I know sorrow and loss and homelessness too* ... I bow my head, and I am full.

Do I stay long in the church? It seems like eternity, all my lifetimes, a completion, a seeing into the essence of things past, present and to come, all complete. But, human as ever, I want something tangible, a *sello* perhaps, my *credencial* is in my pocket, but there is nothing, and no one to guide me to where a *sello* might be obtained. I thank Her for Everything, reluctantly leave Her, wander aimlessly in the elegant crowds, out of sync in the sophisticated surroundings, the material temptations, the gaiety. It is cold and I am discomforted now I am outside. Idly I look in a jeweller's window, oh my, there She is, in gold, far more appropriate for me than a mere scallop shell. And I spend two fortunes on two pendants of La Divina Peregrina, for further along the street I find an exquisite enamel hand painted and gold La Divina Peregrina. Barclays Debit Card obliges both transactions – so there we are! My Secret Agent has a Place in Heaven, probably next to Her.

Home again on the train, my treasures give me the warmest feelings of Something I can't name or fathom. I am wearing them both together on the gold chain I already have round my neck. Apologizing, I remove the not-gold Miraculous Medal and replace it with both La Divina Peregrinas. For the record, Saint Catherine Labouré, to whom the MM appeared, was born Zoé Labouré, it was the Zoé connection I felt akin too – though the French Connection might be more accurate a link for the name Zoé hasn't always been with me. Anyway, She has held me safe until I found La Divina Peregrina, and is generous about my fickleness.

I've always wanted a Mary image that would speak intimately to my solitary journey through life and none really did, not even the icons as pendants. Her image as a *peregrina* sings to me. We speak of the 'pilgrim church on earth'; it assumes a relevance now I connect with Holy Mary as the Divine Pilgrim, Peregrina. In the cloister shop there is an icon image of sorts but it is poorly executed – I will have to do my own.

Bought good food from an artisan grocer, a Spaniard from Bounds Green, from a street I know well from my long ago days with Aunt Alice in London. Tried to siesta, couldn't, came downstairs to see Dane and his cello back from Finisterre going up in the lift; we smile a greeting as the lift ascends. As he is going up an entire orchestra with their instruments is coming down the staircase behind the lift. Another surreal encounter. I follow the orchestra into the courtyard in front of San Martin Pinario where they assemble under an awning and I perch on the wall to hear them play. A film is being made, I am asked to sign a release. It is a performance of fun, inviting different members of the public to act as conductors – the babes in arms look bemused as mini-maestros.

And on that happy and musical note so Endeth my Third Day.

31

Rain and Reflections and a Passing Irritation

27th June 2014. The day dawns in a minor key, rain patters at my window, seagulls wheel over the tiled roof domes, pricks of moving brightness in the sun shafts that pierce the charcoal and leaden skies. This morning I can lie in bed until breakfast, I am weary, achievement is *so* fatiguing...

This attic floor of pilgrims is a distant world of its own, far removed from the 'real' life below. I feel I'm in Gormenghast without the white cats for company. Gone are the days of waking in the clothes of after-shower-yesterday, pinning the damp spare pair of socks to the *mochila*, collecting staff and hat, anointing and swaddling feet to paddle to the boot rack, all in silence, walking out into another new morning, the first yellow arrow a ray of welcome, and off I go.

I amuse myself by reading some of my Camino diaries, now two of them; laugh again at some of the many moments of humour, flip to the photos I have glued in the back of each of them before leaving for the Camino, reflect on the people: Father Bede with HH Darling Lama, a photo taken in Australia during the time Fr Bede was my house guest in 1992; Mrs Tweedie in London; me in India, in sannyasi robes, a pilgrim; Thérèse in Townsville leading the Gyuto monks to the sea to dissolve the sand from their sand mandala; Caroline on her visit to Townsville to find the Black Australia of her childhood dream, there she is standing under the grand waterfall of harlequin bougainvillea tumbling from Thérèse's cliff top garden to the road below; St Francis, the Cimabue image; St Mary Our Lady of Glastonbury, in her red skirt and gold mantle and pale veil, standing and crowned like the Queen of Heaven she is.

In the front I glued tiny copies of my Hare and Hoopoe, and how apt they proved to be at my Epiphany. There is a tiny photo of me, unidentifiable in the distance as anything more than a woman, a woman clothed in the sun; it is archetypal, as it should be. I am alone, walking through the courtyard of the great Monastery of St John of Patmos; responsible for the Twinning in Perpetuity between Glastonbury, the Ancient Sacred Isle of Avalon, and Patmos, the Holy Isle. The two saints, Joseph of Arimathea and St John the Beloved would have known each other, something I was made scintillatingly aware of as I sat in the Cave of the Apocalypse in 2007. A presence in the Cave impressed upon me, as I sat there alone, that linking these two holy places is a task I am beholden to do. I dismiss it of course; I don't do 'public'. The presence and its insistence persisted for three days. I was compelled to approach the Abbot of Patmos. I walked to the Monastery. A large monk, speaking nine languages, wearing a long grey beard and a black chimney pot, a rogue of a man with a chequered and fascinating past including, incredibly, a stint as something professional in the huge and now defunct asylum in Wells, he knew Glastonbury well. He led me to the Abbot, acted as translator. The Abbot and I were in accord, he embraced the link, knew and appreciated the legend of St Joseph of Arimathea and the Holy Thorn, urged me to speak to the Mayor of Glastonbury on my return.

And so it came to pass, a grand five day event for the visiting Patmos delegates, tours and the Tor, Chalice Well and lunch, a gala dinner with all manner of dignitaries present. One of the high-ranking clergy present congratulated me on having brought together at the same table for the first time in 500 years representatives of the three major Christian faiths since the Dissolution of the Monasteries, seriously misnamed the

Reformation. Glastonbury shone with sun and warmth that September of 2009. I had spoken with the Government official responsible for setting up Twinning protocol, unsure how to name our link. She said it had to be a Twinning in Perpetuity, applauded me for creating the first such Twinning in Great Britain; for what else could a link between saints of 2000 years ago be but perpetual? John Michel told me in March he felt that his prophetic book *The Dimensions of Paradise* published forty years earlier had now been redeemed. He would feel privileged, he said, to speak at the Gala Dinner. Three weeks after our conversation John died. His presence remains.

This tiny archetypal photograph of me mirrors chapter twelve of St John: a great sign appeared in the sky, *a woman clothed with the sun*. In the photo, taken from a great distance and without my knowing, I am clothed with the sun, walking in the sunlight between the shadows of the arches. It is not me I see walking through the shadowed centuries of cloistered patriarchy here, but *all* women, women walking in their own Light.

I see my life as a mosaic, nothing appears to link one thing with the next; no rise and rise in a career path; no continuation to even the most remote success; my life's single theme is my Obedience to the Other, a theme invisible to the onlooker. It is a lonely path but sometimes I am blessed to look into the eyes of a fellow pilgrim of the inner way and we recognise each other through the eyes, know each other. These are my friends.

Since 2014 a small number of people have begun an ordinary twinning association between the two places, based on cultural and social ephemera. It has no causal link with saints, nor anything perpetual, twinning association longevity being limited to the committees that uphold them. They are different, these social twinnings, friendships more or less of good will between nations. A Twinning in Perpetuity is a singular event. A woman from the Midlands, having a Jewish connection, but none with Glastonbury or Patmos until after their being twinned in Perpetuity, encouraged the new social twinning. It seemed to me and to a few Patmians that her interest served to promote a personal platform; but that's the Way of the World and we render unto Caesar that which is inevitable: Ἀπόδοτε οὖν τὰ Καίσαρος Καίσαρι καὶ τὰ τοῦ Θεοῦ τῷ Θεῷ. When I return I must address an insult, a public insult and personal to me and the Twinning in Perpetuity. It threw me off balance at the time, but time has passed, my mind has cleared and I can respond to this woman, this oversized cuckoo who can feather her own nest without sullying mine, thank you very much! Lying in bed blissfully horizontal waiting to go down for breakfast has brought up this unfinished business. I am, naturally, riven with faults and failings, they abound, but I've spoken with each over the years, spoken of them to myself, my Higher Self, to Holy Mary, to a good Jungian analyst, and am reconciled to my frailties and humanness. I will give no quarter to guilt when I return home and clear the air. I smile, will add relish to my response to the cuckoo's silly ego. My temporary head-trip fades as I think delicious thoughts of re-arranging an ego ... hers, and in great good humour I shower and dress and skip down four floors and eight flights of stairs to breakfast.

Today I am doing churches and museums, leisurely.

Only a day or so, The End is Nigh...

32

At the End of the Known World

Finisterre – nothing prepared me for this day of surprises at the End of the Known World. Rain fell in torrents throughout the night and right through breakfast and on goes the poncho so I can reach the coach stop which is a ten minute walk away. I am fortunate, not first in the queue, but in the four front seats sit three friends; I claim the fourth seat right there in the front, almost under the little swinging *bruja* who hangs from the rear vision mirror on the windscreen. I set her a task, she who hangs there with her miniature broomstick: *please sweep away all the rainclouds before we reach the end of the world.*

I am grouchy inside, tired. People are late, the guide is stressed, time ticks past the witching hour scheduled for our departure. *Stuff them,* I think darkly, *I would leave them behind. Planes don't wait for no shows,* Satyananda once told us, and the logic of his comment gave me such boldness that years later when I was in Urfa waiting for the coach of tourists to arrive so I could join them for a tour of Harran I waited for seven minutes past the departure time and demanded to go anyway. When I had booked the trip earlier the man said the tour would go even if I was the only person. I pressed the case, reminding the Turkish travel agent of his own words – the Kurd standing behind him laughing hugely and silently at my challenging a Turk, the historical oppressor in their land – and I was given a taxi. All to myself and no extra charge. I sat begum-like in the back all the way to Harran and the eighth century, was gifted a hoopoe feather from a cloudless sky at the temple ruins of the moon god Sin, and given the keys of the Renault 12 by my handsome, chivalrous, Kurd driver when I told him I had the same model car back in Oz. He had seen the hoopoe feather fall, seen the cloudless, birdless blue sky, spoke of special signs and the Eye of Allah, became intensely solicitous of my footfall amongst the jagged and uneven ruins. Back in the office he waxed lyrical to his colleagues of my driving, my negotiating the labyrinthine alleys of Urfa and everyone, including the Turk, was in great good humour. I was given their delicious apple tea, blowtorch sweet, and told the coach had broken down anyway, somewhere east of Nemrut Dağ.

Much too late we leave, the stragglers are a honeymoon couple for whom time is a notion that belongs far beyond their rosy world. Each time we stop for the sightseeing along the way my legs complain at having to get up and walk. Gene and Sandy sit behind me, they are also tired and our couple of days rest has proved our legs far less than infallible. I am more tired than I know. Ponte Maceira, waterfalls, Cee, forgettable Muros, all with a guide whose English is unrecognisable as my mother tongue. Her words delivered as bullet sound-bites without nuance or punctuation render them incomprehensible. A most excellent accent with barely a trace of English ... Was that church bombed or struck by lightning? Did Napoleon rape and pillage or restore and improve? Which war? World War Two, the Spanish Civil or the Christians and Moors? And telling us in English what to look out for on the right as we passed whatever it was two bends back because the Spanish explanation took a kilometre to say ... all rather vexing.

I asked her when was lunch. Uh oh! *Two o'clock,* she snaps. *Two o'clock!* I gasp, remembering breakfast was at seven o'clock. *Lunch in Spain,* she fairly growls, she's obviously met the lunch-at-noon brigade before, *is two o'clock; you are in Spain, we lunch at two o'clock, don't you know. I was in Spain for breakfast* I reply, *but it doesn't stop me being hungry after 5 hours.* Golly, it will be seven hours without food, I feel a coma coming on!

But, here we are at Finisterra. The rain stops; the blueness of the sky astonishing in its clarity. The very earth is different. I step on to it and feel a sizzle, an amalgam of goose bumps, and I am alive. Gone my grouches, gone my grumbles, gone my aches, gone my lurching on the walking stick, I am on the Camino path and it carries me. It is *true*, so many pilgrims say it, the Way will carry you, it is *true*.

The 0.00 kilometres sign on the last milestone is one thing, the Faro de Finisterre another, the lonely Cross a third. Being given the *sello* for the End of the Known World brings an upwelling of tears to all of us who had walked so far knowing our limitations would prevent us the final difficulties of walking the four days to Finisterre. I am so glad I came. I leapt from the coach and fairly hop from craggy rock to boulder to see signs of fire pits and smouldering ashes and then, round a particularly sheer and rugged protrusion, a curl of smoke. Two young men are burning their pilgrim clothes. I congratulate them, they are brimming with light and joy, one asks if he can take a photo of me with my camera at the end of the world. I demur, I have not walked to it, but then, *oh yes please* falls out of my mouth – I am *here!* My gratitude glowed, tears flowed. The two young men are Italians, from that region of Switzerland.

Down then to the town, my spirits transformed, I grin at the tour guide, tell her the place is wonderful, she is Galician, compliments for her country melt stone. She smiles back, we are fine. Sandy and Gene and I choose an empty restaurant on the quay, we are hungry and think the service will be quicker. We learn from the moment we are rationed to portions of bread for two given to three the reason why the restaurant is empty. Gene, the most affable of men, asks for a portion of bread divisible for three and is served with a volley of words in which, *yes of course I'll just cut some more for you,* is not discernible. The dishes are as mean and as measured, poor and pricey. We do not intend to leave a tip. But as we sit alone and obvious in this empty restaurant one of those moments occurs: *Cindy! How lovely!* I call, for here she is, and as pleased to see me. She comes to sit with us awhile. She has not met Sandy or Gene, not once along the 500 miles. Isn't it curious who we meet and who we miss even walking the same path at the same time. Cindy and I had not hoped to meet again after our sharing at breakfast days before, had not bumped into each other, yet here she is. She had caught a local bus to Finisterre yesterday and will walk the long day to Muxia tomorrow. *I promised my body I wouldn't push it anymore but we had a little talk and decided we could manage one more day!* We laugh, swap emails.

Cindy is from Boulder and when she hears I am from Glastonbury laughs and tells Gene, when he commented that Boulder is a bit left of field, that Glastonbury is the last word in way out there and makes Boulder look boring. We hug, take photos, wave goodbye and she calls out to me: *start from Le Puy, your smile will get you through France, a smile speaks twenty languages!*

And so on to Muxia, named for the monks of an 11th century Benedictine monastery. The rock, the sail belonging to the Virgin of the Boat, is clear to see, but no going through the narrow hole nine times for me; Men-an-Tol cured me of crawling through little holes in or under rocks for all time. I love the legend though: St James, Santiago, came here in despair thinking he had failed in his mission and the Blessed Virgin appeared, sailing in to the land in a small barque, to console him and say indeed he hadn't failed at all.

Each one of us feels this to be the true end to our long walk; each of us sits on the sea pounded rocks lost in reverie and sea spray, silently. My pilgrimage is over.

185

33

The Final Farewell

There are new people in rooms adjacent to mine. How can they be so loud? It sounds like they are dismantling the bed, unscrewing the sink – whoops, there goes the wrench crashing to the tiled floor. What *do* they *do?* I can only giggle.

Today I will pack my Opinel knife, my Aussie Barmah, nail file and scissors to post home. I posted them to the hotel in Bilbao two weeks before leaving Glastonbury as I couldn't take them on the flight in my backpack, cabin baggage. The clever hat is able to squash flat, the way it arrived from Australia. I use the walking stick as a 'mobility aid', it isn't a walking pole, and I am allowed to have that with me. Will buy final small gifts today. Cindy wondered if people who walk the Camino more than once are lonely in their home community for the Camino really is a community in motion. When it stops in Santiago only the truest connections will continue. I hope mine will continue, run through my small list of special encounters. Everyone else outran me.

At breakfast a good-looking New Zealand woman asks to sit with me. Rhyll hasn't a drop of Welsh in her veins but chose her name – a Far Memory moment. She does claim Irish though, and conversations, circuitous around the yoghurt and fresh orange juice and breads and cheese and good coffee wind up in Pennant Melangell where I can tell her a 6th century Irish princess left Ireland to become a holy hermit in north Wales. Because of her, Saint Melangell, the Prince of

Powys made all hares protected when the one he was coursing ran into a thicket and his dogs refused to follow. He dismounted, walked through, saw the trembling hare taking refuge with a woman whose sanctity he recognised and thenceforth respected. The hare is a one of the sacred creature of the Old Ways. Rhyll happens to be going to Oxford next year and will explore Powys. She only began her walk in Sarria, with a backpack on wheels, an ordinary cabin case; so difficult, she taxi'd 35 of the 100 kilometres and didn't claim a *Compostela*; she'd come a long way for a short walk. Still sharing stories we walk together to my room.

I dawdle, pack my *mochila*, give Rhyll my hare shirt, a silk talisman printed with pale grey hares which I had found after a dream I had before leaving Glastonbury in which a hare was to accompany me; my rose scarf; it is good to pass these on, I couldn't bring myself to burn them. Things were different in times past when those practices were in place, hostelries weren't blessed with showers and soap barely invented.

The weather is not warm even now, the end of June. I wander listlessly, admire architectural scallop shells, drift into the Parador café for a hot chocolate; it doesn't lift my spirits. The magic has left me. Time to go back to the Cathedral for a final farewell to Santiago.

A surprise – the great silver-cased relic of Santiago greets me in the apse, I am charmed by its very human expression, go up very close, respectfully, wonder why it is here on its bier surrounded by liveried men. I will wait for the Mass and watch the procession. The bells chime the hour, but nothing happens. I wonder why things are not quite as they should be. Time passes. I walk around the crowds, drawn to a focused point amongst the rows of chairs where people are gathered, hunched and murmuring around a collapsed body. Quietly a team of paramedics swiftly appear, a blood transfusion right here as I watch. But the body is carried out under a shroud, face covered, on a stretcher. The solemnity of the music that follows as Mass can then begin adds gravitas to the scene. There is more quiet movement over *there*, and I walk to it, the Botafumeiro is being lowered. Entranced I find a good plinth to perch on, watch the men struggle under the weight of the bier as they process slowly along the nave, disappear into clouds of incense, bring the relic to rest. A handsome couple seem to be a focus. Later I learn the old King abdicated and the young Lovelies, Felipe and Letizia, have come to Santiago for a blessing. They are as lovely a couple as our own Wills and Kate.

I meet up with Gene and Sandy who are far better adapted to leaving tomorrow than I am and we have a last meal together in the Parador bistro. It is beyond superb. I had two starters and no main; sea urchin au gratin, scallops in the lightest of sauces the like of which I've never tasted. Gene has crisp sardines and green beans; knowing I will not eat like this in England I succumb to a small plate and can't finish them. A dessert of spun chocolate so rich and generous follows, but not for me.

The day's gifts do not dispel my feeling of reluctance at returning to Chaingate Court with its mix of human difficulties. Sleep is dreamless. I wake on this final day, say goodbye to my pilgrim room, take my pack down with me to breakfast, thank the waiters, one of whom gives me a hug. With a heart heavy and anchored with unshed tears I walk as if from a long dream out into the rain and down to the local bus to Lavacolla to wait for my flight to Gatwick.

Codicils

Karel emailed after some months, he had many miracles along the Way. The most profound was seeing written in stones and in Dutch: *Linda is here.* He sent me a photo. It wasn't his daughter of course, but as a Sign it took some beating. And in Finisterra the bronze dolphins undid him – he had just heard from his wife that the last photo of his beloved daughter on the camera that finally found its way to his home from the wreckage was of Linda feeding dolphins. His confirmation of Mystery has since sent him on many journeys. Johanna, when I told her later, was delighted her medallion of Our Lady of Finisterre had played a part in Karel's journey.

Cindy emailed that her feet were only a little troubling, but all was well.

Christine took off on more pilgrimages, walking one of the most difficult, Via Francigena, with a diversion to Assisi. Sigeric, Abbot of Glastonbury, walked the Via Francigena from Canterbury in 990. My most favourite of all pilgrim bronzes is by Heather Burnley and stands in Glastonbury Abbey: Sigeric is on his donkey, a ragged child, *ragazzino,* with a beatific smile, is offering him an apple.

I felt inspired, though cautious, to walk again, and tentatively prepared a short walk from Porto. Christina was happy to do it too, from Porto to Santiago. Refugios were rare, and I doubted my capacity. I should have bowed out but an older friend asked me to walk it for her, she would pay for me to stay in modest hotels. I became ill in body, health and temper, triggered by erratic eating times over much longer distances on the Caminho Português. Actually it was hell. Christina, half my age and fit, took the brunt and we parted company. I'm not surprised; I am only surprised I survived at all. It was hell for me as well as she and at the end of it I struggled home to be diagnosed with advanced diabetes. Which explained All.

I confine my perambulations now to the country lanes around Glastonbury; am intensely disciplined about eating every two to three hours to prevent sugar collapse, with its corollary, temper collapse into savagery – a fight/flight symptom of the body's demand for survival. It's a tricky thing, and only those living with it, or with someone who suffers it, appreciate the descent into a personality almost schizoid. I sigh, and make sure of lunch at noon wherever I am and warn my friends, *this is so.*

I left my boots, faithful to the prediction they would last a thousand miles, outside the Pilgrims Office in Santiago; left them with their cheery polka dot ribbons still tied to their laces in gratitude. And my feet? Well, my feet are my best friends and we speak together regularly. My pilgrim feet will carry me to the very End.